Alberta's Political Pioneers: A Biographical Account of the United Farmers of Alberta

United Farmers of Alberta in the Political Life of the Province

1921-1935

Mardon, Austin A. (Austin Albert)
Alberta's political pioneers : a biographical account of the
United Farmers of Alberta / author: Austin Mardon ; editors: Emerson Csorba, Spencer Dunn, and Justin Selner.

ISBN 978-1-897472-12-5

1. United Farmers of Alberta--Biography. 2. Alberta--Politics
and government. I. Csorba, Emerson II. Dunn, Spencer
III. Selner, Justin IV. Title.

HD1486.C3M37 2010 334'.683 C2010-905246-3

Acknowledgements

Any study of this sort is dependent upon the support and efforts of a wide variety of people. The authors would like to thank the staff at the Provincial Archives of Alberta, the Legislative Library of Alberta, and the Office of the Chief Electoral Officer of Alberta for all of their assistance and encouragement. They would also like to thank the staff of the Historic Sites and Archives Service, Alberta Community Development, the Edmonton Public Library, the Calgary Public Library, the Lethbridge Public Library, and many other historical sources. A special thanks to Spencer Dunn, Justin Selner, and Emerson T. Csorba, who were all very helpful in typing the manuscript, and to whose language and editorial skills were a great asset. Any errors or omissions remain the responsibility of the authors.

Alberta's Political Pioneers: A Biographical Account of the United Farmers of Alberta

United Farmers of Alberta in the Political Life of the Province

1921-1935

E Mardon & A Mardon

Edited by Justin Selner, Spencer Dunn & Emerson Csorba

Edmonton, Albert, Canada 2010

Dedicated to:
May Gertrude Knowler, the imagination for the Historical Project

TABLE OF CONTENTS

Preface

The essence of the true democratic process is that individuals are selected from the collective whole of a society to act on behalf of that collective society in the area of political governance. In examining the process of governance, we sometimes forget the representatives that are elected are only part of the democratic arena. Within many societies, the losers do not accept their defeat gently and with grace.

For democracy to continue to exist, these defeated candidates must be willing to accept the will of the people as expressed through the ballot box and selection of candidates.

Historically, in many societies disintegration of the political process and the transfer of power is instigated by losers in the voting process taking up arms.

The losers should be included in a history of the political landscape of Alberta for the above reasons: these losing candidates are a distinct part of the political process and important for our society's continued smooth functioning. It is only with their peaceful acceptance of 'the will of the people' that our political institutions continue to exist. The other assumption of our work is that the individual life history of each politician distinctly affects the manner in which they chart the course of the state. As Lord Thomas Macauley, the 19th century British historian, states, "History is ultimately biography." The Marxist historical analyst would question the validity of individual biographies. In our view, by developing taxonomies

General Introduction

The rich lands of the Province of Alberta were claimed in quarter section lots by pioneer settlers in the thousands during the first decade of the twentieth century. The homesteaders soon became farmers and established themselves in small groups and organizations for helping each other and collectively meeting the problems of marketing their cattle and grain.

In 1909, the United Farmers of Alberta was established by an amalgamation of the Canadian Society of Equity and the Alberta Farmers Association. James Speakman was elected the first president of the farm organization.

The members resented particularly the contrast between the low prices for their products on the world market and the high prices they had to pay for manufactured good sheltered behind the Canadian tariff wall. They were also concerned about other social and economic issues, including living conditions in remote rural areas.

In 1915 the U.F.A. organized the United Farm Women of Alberta, which energetically promoted the cause of prohibition and campaigned for women's suffrage. The Legislature gave women the vote in 1916. A year later, two women were members of the Legislature.

It was not until 1921 that the U.F.A. became totally involved in both federal and provincial politic. Henry Wise Wood, an American farmer and preacher, was elected the agricultural organization's president in 1916. While he held this position for fifteen years, Wise Wood was a strong believer in the need for Christian ethics in economic activities. Conversely, the Carstairs wheat farmer was accused of promoting a "Soviet" or group style of politics.

Wood was the man with a dream and through grass root U.F.A. movement he toppled the Liberal provincial government of Charles Stewart in the 1921 General Election. The U.F.A. did not run candidates in the cities of Edmonton and Calgary or the coal mining constituencies of Lethbridge, Rocky Mountain, and Edson.

Wood himself refused to become the premier. At a Calgary U.F.A. convention in August 1921, Herbert Greenfield, a Westlock farmer, was selected the movements leader and was asked to form a government by Lieutenant Governor Robert G. Brett. Premier Greenfield's cabinet included Alex Ross, a Calgary Labour member, as Minister of Municipal Affairs and John E. Brownlee, the long-time solicitor of the U.F.A., as the Attorney General. The other members had been directors or prominent, active, and vocal farmers. The former president of the U.F.A., Irene Parlby, was included in the executive council.

This farm organization governed the province for 14 years.

In 1935 this unique government was defeated by the Great Depression, personal scandals, and the Social Credit movement of William (Bible Bill) Aberhart.

In many ways this was the golden age of the parliamentary system in Alberta. The membership of the Legislature comprised the most unusual group of men and women ever to sit in a Legislature at any time in the history of Canada. Biographical histories of U.F.A. members and their allies who were sent to the House of Commons are included in this monograph.

Henry Wise Wood was called the Moses of Alberta farmers. Let us not forget him or his followers, as their lives are a vital part of our political history.

BIOGRAPHICAL HISTORIES

ADSHEAD, Herbert Bealey

Born October 17, 1862 near Manchester, England, son of Nathaniel Adshead and Jane Roberts.

Educated at Manchester Grammar School, he came to Canada as a sixteen-year-old youth and settled near Ottawa, where he was the accountant for the Gilmour and Rathburn Lumber Company. Later, he attended Ottawa Normal School, qualifying as a teacher. In 1882, he married Ellen Unwin of Madoc, Ontario, a relation of the British publishers – the Unwin Brothers.

Adshead came to the District of Alberta, N.W.T. in 1898, where he taught school and homesteaded in the Olds district. After farming for fourteen years, he moved to Calgary in 1912. At this time, he wrote a book entitled "Pioneer Days."

Active in civic affairs, Adshead served as a Calgary Liberal alderman for three years before unsuccessfully running as the Liberal Mayoralty candidate in 1921. He was only defeated by ten votes.

Interested in provincial politics, Herbert B. Adshead unsuccessfully contested the five-member Calgary constituency in 1921 as an Independent Farmer candidate. In a field of twenty candidates, he placed fourteenth.

Turning to federal politics, Adshead, running as an Independent Labour candidate, successfully contested the Calgary East riding in the 1926 election. He defeated Conservative incumbent Fred Davis by a 1,575 vote margin. He sat in Parliament for four years as a private member on the opposition benches. In his re-election bid in the 1930 federal election, Adshead was defeated by Conservative Dr. George Stanley. He then retired from politics.

He died May 2, 1932 in Calgary at the age of seventy.

ALLEN, Hugh Wright

Born April 30, 1889 in Stella, Ontario, son of William Allen and Mary Wright, and grandson of Scottish immigrants, he was educated at Stella and the Kingston Collegiate Institute. He trained first as a teacher before taking employment as a chemist with Ontario Power Company at Tweed for three years. Allen was engaged in the manufacturing of high explosives. In 1911, he was among the first wave of pioneer settlers to move into the Peace River Country. He became a prominent farmer of the Wembly district and President of the United Farmers of Alberta local for many years. The hamlet of Huallen is named after him.

In 1921, Allen failed to win the U.F.A. nomination for the provincial Peace River constituency, losing to Donald M. Kennedy. However, Hugh W. Allen returned as the U.F.A. member for the provincial Peace River constituency in 1926. He sat in the Legislature for nine years. In 1934 Premier Reid appointed Allen to the Cabinet as Minister of Lands, Mines, and Municipalities. In 1935 he was defeated and subsequently began a career in Peace River's agro-economic development. He contributed to the formation of the Alberta Livestock Cooperative in 1940 where he served as President. In 1967, Hugh Wright Allen was inducted into the Alberta Agriculture Hall of Fame.

In 1911, he married Mabel Sill of Tweed, Ontario. They had no children. Hugh Allen died March 3, 1972 in Grande Prairie.

ANDREWS, Albert George

Born September 13, 1881 in Berkampstead, Hartfordshire, England, son of David Andrews. Albert George Andrews was educated at Batterseas's St. John College and worked for fifteen years in England as a schoolmaster. After coming to Alberta in 1910, he taught in rural schools for seven years before becoming a prominent farmer of the Sedgewick district. He served as a Flagstaff Municipal Councilor for three years and as a President of the U.F.A. local for several years.

Albert George Andrews was returned as the U.F.A. member for the provincial Sedgewick constituency in the July 10, 1922 by-election. He sat in the Legislature for 13 years as a private member on the government side of the chamber.

In 1941, Andrews served on the Alberta School Trustee Association Executive, and from 1948 to 1950 he served as a member of the Canadian Trustee Association.

In 1913, he married Margaret Edmunds of Stranraer, Scotland. They had two sons and two daughters. Albert G. Andrews died November 1, 1916 in Sedgewick.

Source: Canadian Parliamentary Guide (1926), p. 530

ANGELO, John

Of Italian descent, John Angelo became an Athabasca farmer. In 1921, he unsuccessfully ran as the U.F.A. candidate for the provincial Athabasca constituency, placing second to Liberal incumbent George Mills.

Source: Canadian Parliamentary Guide (1926), p. 530

AXELSON, Carl Henning

Born October 7, 1877 in Mjolby, Sweden, Carl Henning Axelson migrated to the United States as a young man. Although educated in Sweden, Axelson became active in the Trade Union Movement as a follower of Daniel DeLeon, the American Socialist leader. Later he joined the Socialist Labor Party. In 1910, he homesteaded in a Swedish community in the Bingville district near Medicine Hat. He became a successful farmer, active in the United Farmers of Alberta for many years. In 1930, Axelson ran against Henry Wise Wood for the presidency of the U.F.A. but was defeated.

Carl H. Axelson became one of the most prominent farm leaders in the province. He twice unsuccessfully ran as the U.F.A. candidate: first for the federal Medicine Hat riding in 1926 and again for the federal Athabasca riding in the March 21, 1932 by-election. In 1926, he placed third in a field of three candidates, garnering 2,081 (24.44%) out of a total of 8,513 votes. Liberal member Frederick William Gershaw won with 4,206 votes (49.41%).

In the 1930s Axelson founded the Workers Unity League. He travelled widely across the country delivering impassioned socialist speeches and advocated for radical changes in the economic system. In the spring of 1932 he toured the Soviet Union and later lectured on what he had seen. This included introducing Russian Methods of collective agriculture into Canada.

Axelson was found dead August 15, 1932, hanging from a rope attached to a beam in the barn of his farm in Bingville. Dr. Oliver Boyd, coroner, stated that it was suicide. He had been in financial difficulties for three years in the operation of his farm, which was given as a possible cause. He died at age fifty-five.

BAILEY, William Henry

Born November 9, 1889 in Mason County, Michigan, son of Philip Enos Bailey and Josephine Major. He was of United Empire Loyalist stock on his mother's side. Educated at Ludington, Michigan, William Bailey worked at various jobs including store-clerking and lumber milling. At Scott, Saskatchewan, he worked for a time clearing the land for the federal experimental farm. In 1991, he and his brother were among the first pioneer settlers to move into the Peace River Country, where they homesteaded in the Berwyn district near Fairview. It is here he became a prominent farmer.

William Henry Bailey was returned as the U.F.A. member for the provincial Peace River constituency in 1930. He sat in the Legislature for five years as a private member on the government side of the chamber. He was defeated in 1935 and returned to his farm. He continued to operate his farm until he retired to Edmonton.

In 1916 he married Mattie McAuley of Peace River. They had three daughters. He was also a member of the United Church.

William H. Bailey died December 7, 1975 in Berwyn.

BAKER, Percival

Born on January 11, 1867 in York County, Ontario to Jacob Baker and educated in Ontario, Percival Baker attended the College of the Bible (Kentucky University) at Lexington, graduating in the class of 1889. He spent eleven years as a farm hand in Ontario and another twenty years as a minister of the gospel, including eleven years at Guelph. In 1908, he settled near Ponoka, where he farmed and preached on a regular basis.

He was selected as the United Farmers of Alberta Director for Strathcona in 1916, and was elected third Vice-President in 1918. Percival Baker was defeated as an Independent for the provincial Ponoka constituency in 1913, losing to Liberal incumbent William A. Campbell. Eight years later he was returned as the U.F.A. member for the provincial Ponoka constituency on July 18, 1921.

A week before the election he was badly injured by a falling tree while felling trees on his farm. Two days after the election, on July 20, 1921, he died in the Royal Alexandra Hospital in Edmonton. He was survived by his wife, Susan Amanda Page, five sons and two daughters.

BAKER, Perren Earle

Born August 10, 1877 in Blenheim, Ontario, son of Albert C. Baker and Sarah J. Gillies. Both parents were Canadians of Scottish descent.

Educated at Sarnia, Baker attended McGill University, graduating in Arts. He then did post-graduate work at Chicago. From 1906 to 1909 he was an unordained minister in Illinois.

Coming to Alberta in 1910, Perren Baker became a leader in the farming community. In 1905 he married Blanche Randall of Grimsby, Ontario. They had two sons and a daughter. His wife died in 1916 and he was re-married to Edna Brown of Vancouver in 1920.

Baker was an active member of the United Farmers of Alberta. In early 1921, he unsuccessfully contested the federal Medicine Hat nomination at the U.F.A. convention. Robert Gardiner was named and went on to win. In July 1921, Perren Earle Baker was returned as one of the two members for the provincial Medicine Hat constituency. He sat in the Legislature for 14 years, all of them as the Minister of Education. In 1935, he was defeated by Social Creditor A.W. Flamme. Baker then retired from politics to his 1,800 acre wheat farm.

Perren E. Baker died February 13, 1974 in Vancouver at the

elderly age of ninety-six.

(See The Canadian Who's Who, 1939).

Source: Canadian Parliamentary Guide (1926), p. 530-531

BARNES, Samuel Augustus Gordon

Born August 10, 1875 in Warwick Township, Ontario, son of Samuel D. Barnes and Lois Hagle. His father's ancestors had come from Wiltshire, England in 1800 to pioneer in Upper Canada.

Educated in Strathroy Collegiate Institute, Barnes attended Toronto Normal School, qualifying as a teacher. He continued his studies at the University of Manitoba, graduating in 1903 with an Arts degree. He taught in Saskatchewan from 1897 to 1901.

S.A. Gordon Barnes came to the District of Alberta, N.W.T. in 1902. He settled in Edmonton, where he became a prominent insurance agent.

Active in community affairs, he was active in the Teacher's Association, advocating for improved working conditions and adequate teacher salaries. Moreover, Barnes was also active in the Temperance Movement in Alberta that resulted in prohibition.

Interested in politics, S.A. Gordon Barnes was a staunch Liberal in his youth. In 1917, he became involved with the Labor Movement. He unsuccessfully contested the six member Edmonton constituency in 1930 as a Labor candidate. In a field of seventeen, he placed tenth.

Turning to federal politics, S.A. Gordon was defeated in the Edmonton West riding in the December 1921 general election.

In later years, Barnes converted to the Social Credit. Prominent in the Social Credit League, Aberhart named him as one of the party's Edmonton candidates in the summer of 1935. In the 1935 August general election, Barnes was elected, standing second in the popular vote, behind the Liberal Alberta leader, W.R. Howson.

In 1937, he joined the so-called Social Credit "insurgents" who unsuccessfully attempted to force Premier Aberhart to resign. He then crossed the floor of the Legislature to sit as an Independent. In 1940, he ran unsuccessfully as an Independent Progressive. Samuel Augustus Gordon Barnes died on April 14, 1941.

BEVINGTON, George Elza

Born January 4, 1874 in Grant Cons Country, Missouri. Educated in Grant Cons Country. As a young man, he had numerous jobs including freighting, mining and panning for gold. In 1898 he took part in the Gold Rush at the Klondike gold field in the Yukon.

Bevington came to Alberta in 1906 and settled permanently at Winterburn, west of Edmonton, where he became a prominent farmer. He brought with him registered Holsteins from Ontario to improve his dairy herd, and in later years, he built a cheese factory. Unfortunately, in 1922 the herd was infected with bovine tuberculosis and was forced to be destroyed.

Active in the United Farmers of Alberta Movement, George Elza Bevington served on the Executive for several years. However, he twice unsuccessfully ran as the U.F.A. candidate; first for the federal Jasper-Edson riding in 1935, and again for the provincial Stony Plain constituency in 1940.

In 1945 he sold his Winterburn farm and retired to live in Edmonton, where he eventually died on January 22, 1965.

Source: Canadian Parliamentary Guide (1936), (1938), p.293

BOUTILLIER, Arthur Moreu

Born October 16, 1869 in Halifax, Nova Scotia. Son of Esrom Boutillier, a Frenchman, and Anne Spear, of Irish decent, Boutillier was educated at the Halifax Academy. He came to the District of Alberta, N.W.T. in 1890, and homesteaded near Soda Lake, where he became a well-known farmer. He served as the Treasurer for the Eagle municipal district for many years.

Arthur Moreu Boutillier was returned as the U.F.A. member for the federal Vegreville riding in 1925. He sat in the House of Commons for one year. In 1926 he did not seek re-election, but returned to his farm.

Boutillier married twice: first in 1893 to Wilhemia Busch of

Halifax. They had several children before she died in 1913. He was remarried in 1914 to Laura White. They had two sons, Harry Roy and Robert. H. Boutillier, unsuccessfully ran for the federal Vegreville riding in 1940. He later became a prominent farm leader in the province.

Source: Canadian Parliamentary Guide (1926), p.292

BRETON, Douglas Corney

Born November 25, 1883 in Simmons Town, South Africa, son of William E. Breton and Alice Dudoit his French wife. His father was a former Inspector General of Loyalists and fleets of the Royal British Navy while his mother was the daughter of the French consul to the Hawaiian Islands. He was educated at Portsmouth Grammar School.

Breton came to the District of Alberta, N.W.T. in 1904, and became a prominent Leduc farmer and merchant. During World War I, he enlisted in the British Army and saw active service on the Western Front, both in India and Afghanistan, as a Captain. The town of Breton, Alberta was named after Douglas Corney Breton in 1927.

Douglas Corney Breton was returned as the U.F.A. member for the provincial Leduc constituency in 1926. He sat in the Legislature for four years as a private member on the government side of the chamber. Breton was defeated in his re-election bid in 1935 and returned to his farm.

In 1920 he married Dorothy Blanche, daughter of M.E.P. Frort, O.B.E. They had two children. Within some time, Breton moved to England.

Source: Canadian Parliamentary Guide (1928), p.346

BROWN, Samuel

Born November 11, 1872 in Ballymony, County Antrim, Ireland, he was raised on a farm. Educated at Ballymount, he served as a carpenter's apprentice at Bushmills. After working in the Belfort shipyards, Brown crossed the Atlantic and went to Nebraska in search of free land. This was largely because all of the homesteads had been occupied and the cheap land gone.

Samuel Brown came to the District of Alberta, N.W.T. in 1904 and homesteaded in the Blackie district. With the crop disaster of 1906, he moved to High River, where he was appointed the local peace officer and then became a successful contractor. In 1911, he returned to his Blackie farm while also managing the Crown Lumber Company. During this time, he became a prominent farmer.

Active in the U.F.A. movement, he served as the Secretary of the local branch of the farm organization for many years. Samuel Brown was returned as the U.F.A. member for the provincial High River constituency in 1921. He sat in the Legislature for nine years as a private member on the government side of the chamber. In 1930 the High River constituency was combined with Okotoks constituency as Okotoks-High River. Brown did not contest Cabinet Minister George Hoadley for the nomination but rather, retired from politics. In 1900 he married Jane McIlroy, formerly of Ulster. They had a daughter and two sons. The elder son, Sam Brown Junior, unsuccessfully ran as a Progressive Conservative for the provincial Okotoks-High River constituency in 1963.

Samuel Brown died in 1951 in Edmonton.

Source: Canadian Parliamentary Guide (1926), p. 535

BROWNLEE, B.A., Y.C. John Edward

Born August 27, 1884 in Port Ryerse, Ontario, son of William J. Brownlee and Christian Shaw. His grandfather Edward James Brownlee migrated from Ulster as a young man. His father was a small town merchant and Methodist teacher. Educated in Sarnia, he then attended the Sarnia Normal School where he qualified as a teacher. Brownlee taught at Bradford for three and a half years. In 1904 he entered the University of Toronto. He graduated with an Art degree in 1908.

After a year of travelling throughout the Prairie Provinces, Brownlee settled in Calgary where he articled as a law student in the legal firm of Lougheed and Bennett. After he was admitted to the Alberta Bar in 1912, Brownlee established a Calgary law firm. In 1917 he became the Legal Advisor and General Counsel of the United Farmers of Alberta and the United Grain Growers of Winnipeg. He became a close confident of U.F.A. President Henry Wise Wood, and rapidly became one of the most influential individuals in the powerful farm organization. After the U.F.A. elected a majority of members in the July 1921 Alberta election, President Wood wanted Brownlee to become the Premier.

However, many farmers did not want to be led by a lawyer and selected Herbert Greenfield as the party's leader in the Legislature. Premier Greenfield appointed John E. Brownlee as the Attorney General. Brownlee entered the House by acclimation in the Ponoka by-election, caused by the sudden death of Percival Baker.

In 1923 he successfully opposed radical financial resolutions that he perceived would threaten provincial credit. Brownlee was Wood's choice for the premiership; he succeeded to that office in November, 1925, when Greenfield resigned. On June 5, 1926, Brownlee resigned his position as Attorney General. During his administration the provincially-owned and operated Alberta and Great Waterways Railway and the Edmonton, Dunvegan and British Columbia Railway were sold to the Canadian Pacific Railway and the Canadian National Railway. Furthermore, control of Alberta's resources was transferred to the province by the federal government. Brownlee played an important part in these negotiations that ended a controversy which had existed since 1905. Thus, it is evident that Brownlee managed to make an indelible mark on the future of Alberta.

Brownlee's political career ended in a widely publicized scandal on July 10, 1934, when he was sued for seduction of an eighteen-year-old girl. He was succeeded by Richard G. Reid. The writ had been issued through the Supreme Court channels and claimed unstated damages and costs. The suit had been entered by Allen C. MacMillan, father of the girl, Vivian MacMillan, and the girl herself who was employed as a stenographer at the Government Buildings. The civil action, in which the stated sum of $20,000 was claimed from Brownlee, was heard in the latter part of June. It was concluded on July 1, the jury of six finding in favor of the plaintiff and awarding

$10,000 to Miss MacMillan and $5,000 to her father. On June 30, the day before the conclusion of the case, the judge dismissed an $8,000 counter-claim of Premier Brownlee. In this counter-claim, Brownlee attempted to charge Vivian MacMillan and John Coldwell, a third-year student at the University of Alberta, who had proposed marriage to Miss MacMillan, with conspiracy to obtain money. On July 4, Mr. W.C. Ives, who presided, rendered his judgment, dismissing action with costs, which overruled the jury's verdict. Under the judgment, the MacMillans were required to pay the legal costs of Brownlee as well as their own. An appeal was launched which concluded with the Judicial Committee of the Privy Council, in 1940, sustaining the original award.

Immediately after the jury's verdict, Premier Brownlee rendered his resignation to the Lieutenant-Governor. However, he retained his seat in the Legislature, but was defeated by Mrs. Edith Rogers in the general election the following year. He then returned to his law practice. Brownlee later became manager of the United Grain Growers, a farmer's co-operative. He retired in 1958, but held the position with the United Grain Growers up until two weeks prior to his death.

Brownlee died at the age of seventy-six on July 15, 1961. He was a Methodist.

(See: The Canadian Who's Who, 1958)

Source: Canadian Parliamentary Guide (1935), p.365

BUCKLEY, John Charles

Born November 26, 1863 in Enniskerry County, Wicklow, Ireland, son of Henry Buckley and Maria Louisa Griffiths. He belonged to an Anglo-Irish family with property. Educated at Disraeli's College, Carlow. For 20 years Buckley looked after the family estate. He also served on the Poor Law Board for nine years. In 1906 he came to Alberta and became a prominent Gleichen farmer.

John C. Buckley was returned as the U.F.A. member for the provincial Gleichen constituency in 1921. He sat in the Legislature for

14 years in which he served as the party whip. However, in 1935 he placed second, losing to Social Creditor Issac McCune. Following his loss, Buckley returned to his farm.

In 1884 he had married his cousin Susan, daughter of Richard H. Buckley of Ballybrow, Enniskerry. They had five daughters and three sons. One of his daughters, Beatrice Georgina "Bee" Buckley, married Humphrey M. Parlby, the only son of Irene Parlby, the U.F.A. member for Lacombe.

John C. Buckley died in February 1942 in Calgary. He was Anglican.

Source: Canadian Parliamentary Guide (1935), p. 336

CAMERON, Donald

Born September 16, 1869 in Wood End, Scotland, son of John Cameron and Mary McNicol. He was of Scottish descent. Educated at Glencoe, Cameron then trained for the Civil Service. For five years he was a foreman shipwright with the British Admiralty at Hong Kong. In 1906, he came to Alberta and became a well known Elnora farmer.

Donald Cameron was returned as the U.F.A. member for the provincial Innisfail constituency in 1921. He sat in the Legislature for 14 years as a private member on the government side of the chamber. In 1935 he did not seek re-election, rather retiring from politics at the age of sixty-five. His son Donald Cameron became a senator in the 1950s.

CARSON, Samuel Allen

Born June 3, 1870 in Vernon, Ontario, son of Oliver Cardon and Isabella Allen. While educated in Vernon, he came to the District of Alberta, N.W.T. as a young man and homesteaded near Namao. Carson became a well-known pioneer farmer. In 1898 he married Lorreta J. Maxfield, formerly of Charlottetown P.E.I. They had two sons and two daughters.

Active in community affairs, he was elected Chairman of the Sturgeon School Board in 1907, a position he held for twenty years.

Carson also served as Secretary-Treasurer for the United Farmers of Alberta, Namao local, for many years.

Samuel Allen Carson was returned as the U.F.A. member for the provincial Sturgeon constituency in 1921. He sat in the Legislature for fourteen years as a private member on the government side of the House. In 1935, he did not seek re-election, retiring from politics at the age of sixty-five.

Samuel Carson died February 27, 1949. He was a Methodist.

CHORONOHUS, Michael

Born March 10, 1888 in Russ Banilla, Galicia in Eastern Europe, son of John Choronohus who was a minor Russian official and Justice of the Peace in Ukraine for many years. He was educated at Russ Banilla.

Choronohus came to the District of Alberta, N.W.T. as a child with his parents in 1900, and the family settled near Desjarlais. He was a prominent Desjarlais farmer who was active in the U.F.A. Movement. He served as a reeve of the Eagle Municipal district for three years. As well, he made a study of the economic condition of agriculture.

Michael Choronohus unsuccessfully ran as the U.F.A. candidate for the provincial Whitford constituency in 1921. However, the courts declared this election void due to irregularities. Michael Choronohus was returned as the U.F.A. member for the provincial Whitford constituency in the July 10, 1923 by-election. He sat in the Legislature for three years as a private member on the government side of the chamber. In 1926 he did not seek re-election, but rather retired from politics.

In 1910 he had married Paraska Luchak of Hamlin, Alberta. They had a son and two daughters. He was a member of the Greek Orthodox Church.

He died in 1946 in Edmonton.

CLAYPOOL, Austin Bingley

Born April 13, 1887 at Muncie, Indiana, son of Frank C.

Claypool. Educated at the University of South Tennessee.

Claypool came to Alberta as a young man in 1907 to homestead. He became a prominent farmer and cattle breeder in the Swalwell district. In 1911 he married Elma Suick, daughter of John C. Suick of Muncie.

Austin Bingley Claypool was returned as the U.F.A. member for the provincial Didsbury constituency in 1921. He sat in the Legislature for 14 years as a private member on the government side of the chamber. While in the House, he acted as Chairman of the Agriculture Committee. He was also active in provincial livestock organizations. In 1935 he placed second, losing to Social Creditor, E.P. Foster, who became an M.L.A. for Didsbury in the Legislative Assembly until 1940.

Turning to federal politics, Austin Bingley Claypool, running as a Liberal, unsuccessfully contested the Bow River riding in the 1940 general election. He placed second, losing to Social Credit incumbent C.E. Johnston.

In 1942 he retired to Muncie Indiana on the death of his father. He died June 4, 1956 as a result of injuries suffered in an automobile accident in Muncie. He was a Protestant.

CONNER, Maurice Joy

Born November 30, 1869 in Afton, Iowa, son of Thomas Conner and Helen Afred. Conner was of Irish-English stock. Educated at Afton, he trained as an Evangelical minister and was a minister for many years. He was a man of frank, independent character, thrifty and energetic, and active in public affairs. In 1892, he married Margaret, daughter of William Cooper of Ellston, Iowa. He was a Methodist minister from 1894 to 1912.

Conner came to Alberta with many of his parishioners in 1907 and homesteaded in the Warner district. He became a prominent dry land farmer, owning eleven sections. Notably, his sections were one of the largest and most successful farming operations in the district. Conner also served as a Methodist minister from 1894 to 1912 and was responsible for the building of the Warner Evangelical Church.

Maurice J. Conner was returned as the U.F.A. member for the

provincial Warner constituency in 1921, defeating businessman Frank S. Leffingwell in the process. He sat in the Legislature for 14 years as a government backbencher. In the Legislature he was a vocal U.F.A. backbencher who was often critical of government policies that did not appeal to him. He sat in the House for fourteen years. In 1935, he failed to win the U.F.A. nomination, losing it to Wilbert Stevens and proceeded to retire from politics at the age of sixty-six.

In 1892, he married in Iowa. He had five daughters, one of whom married Dean Gundlock, MP for Lethbridge, 1958-1972. His grandson, Emile Gundlock was an unsuccessful candidate in the provincial election. Maurice Conner died May 9, 1937 in Lethbridge.

COOK, Earl Goodwin

Born November 9, 1881 in Woodburn, Ontario, son of James Cook and Charlotte Merritt. He was of Scotch-Irish descentand educated at Pelham.

He came to the District of Alberta, N.W.T. in 1902 as a young man and became a well known Pincher Creek Station farmer.

Earl G. Cook was returned as the U.F.A. member for the provincial Pincher Creek constituency in 1921. He sat in the Legislature for five years as a private member on the government side of the chamber. On two occasions, 1930 and 1931, he failed in his re-election bids.

In 1905 Cook married Margaret Francis Willock of Pincher Creek. They had three sons and two daughters: Wilfred, Alma, Gladys, Bert and James. Earl Goodwin Cook served as President of the Pincher Coop Association for 14 years until his retirement in 1955.

Earl G. Cook died April 20, 1966. He was a Methodist.

COOK, John Ernest

Born July 3, 1890 in Silver Water, Manitouln Island, Ontario. Educated at Omemee, he attended normal school, qualifying as a teacher. Cook taught in Ontario, before he eventually came to Alberta in 1908, where he taught at Three Hills. After working as a journalist and pioneering in the Peace River Country, he purchased a farm near

Conjuring Creek.

John E. Cook unsuccessfully ran as the U.F.A. candidate for the provincial Leduc constituency in 1935.

COOTE, George Gibson

Born August 18, 1880 in Oakville, Ontario, son of C.W. Coote, a Canadian of Irish descent and Mary Harcus, his wife of Scotch blood. He was educated in Oakville and later became an accountant, bank manager, farmer and politician.

Coming to Alberta as a young man in 1906, Coote became a prominent Cayley farmer. In 1910 he married Jennette McKinnon of Nanton and they had two sons.

George G. Coote was returned the Progressive (U.F.A.) member for the federal Macleod riding in 1921, winning in a field of four contestants. He sat in the House of Commons for 14 years. In 1935 he was defeated by Social Creditor Rev. Ernest George Hansell. In 1936 he was named a Director of the Bank of Canada. Coote was a member of the "Ginger Group" of MPs in the 1920s and 1930s. He also served as Director of the Alberta Wheat Pool from 1936 to 1952 and was Secretary-Treasurer of the Canadian Chamber of Agriculture from 1938 to 1939.

Coote died on November 24, 1959.

(See: The Canadian Who's Who, 1936)

COURSIER, Dr. Heber Leon

Born in Revelstoke, B.C. of French descent in 1893. Coursier was educated in Revelstoke and attended the University of Toronto, graduating in Dentistry in 1916. During World War I, he enlisted in the Canadian Army Medical Corps and served as a dentist on the Western Front. In 1922, he established a dental practice in Wainwright. Active in community affairs, he further served for three years on the town council.

Dr. Heber L. Coursier unsuccessfully ran as a U.F.A. candidate for the provincial Wainwright constituency in 1935.

Coursier died in 1989.

CRITCHLOW, Hugh

A successful Barrhead farmer, who in 1907 took land along the Klondike Trail. In 1910, Hugh Critchlow partnered with Jason Cason to build a post office.

In the 1936 Edmonton Municipal Election, Critchlow ran for the position of Public School Trustee and finished seventh in a field of seven candidates, amassing 2,858 votes compared to winner Frederick Casselman's 14,301.

A C.C.F. supporter, Hugh Critchlow unsuccessfully contested the federal riding of Jasper-Edson in 1940, losing to New Democrat Walter Frederick Kuhl. Critchlow amassed 2,102 votes, whereas Kuhl received 6,363 votes.

During the campaign, Critchlow said that the national C.C.F. party had instigated and had been behind every worthwhile reform in Ottawa, including the establishment of the old age pension scheme. He married Helen Asbury in 1926 and they had three children.

CROSS, Charles Wilson

Born November 30, 1872 in Madoc Hastings County, Ontario, son of Thomas Cross and Marie Mouncey. His father, a native of Aberdeen, was a wealthy Madoc merchant.

Educated at Upper Canada College, he attended the University of Toronto and obtained a Law degree at Osgoode Hall.

Cross came to the District of Alberta, N.W.T. in 1897, and settled in Edmonton where he became a prominent lawyer for the next twenty three years. For several years, he was a member of the legal firm of Short, Cross, Biggar and Ewing.

In 1900 he married Annie L. Linde. They had a son, Thomas Cross who became an Alberta judge and two daughters, one of whom married S.T. Bigelow.

Interested in provincial politics, Charles Wilson Cross successfully contested the Edmonton constituency in the 1905 election and sat as a member of the first Alberta Legislature with Premier Rutherford. Premier Rutherford took him into his first Cabinet as the Attorney General. Cross held this position until he resigned on March 9, 1910, during the railway scandal that toppled the Rutherford administration. Premier Arthur L. Sifton reappointed Cross the Attorney General in May 4, 1913 and he held this post until August 23, 1918. Charles Cross sat in the Legislature for twenty years; the last four on the opposition side of the chamber after the U.F.A. formed the government in 1921.

In 1925, C.W. Cross resigned his seat in the Legislature in order to enter federal politics and was succeeded by Christopher Pattinson. In 1925 he defeated incumbent Donald Ferdinand Kellner to claim Athabasca for the Liberals, but lost in a rematch to the same man a year later. He is the only member of the Legislature to represent two constituencies at the same time. In the 1913 general election, he returned as both the member for Edson and the member for Edmonton.

He died June 2, 1928.

CULLE, James M.

James M. Culle became a High Prairie farmer. However, he unsuccessfully ran as the U.F.A. candidate for the provincial Grouard constituency in the July 11, 1924 by-election. He placed second, losing to Liberal L.A. Giroux.

DAVIDSON, William McCartney

Born November 12, 1872 in Hillier, Prince Edward County, Ontario, son of James C. Davidson and Sarah McCartney Davidson. His ancestors were of United Empire Loyalist stock.

Educated at St. Catherine Collegiate Institute, Davidson attended the University of Toronto, graduating in Arts in 1892. He worked as a parliamentary reporter for The Toronto World and The Toronto Star from 1893 to 1901, when he became the Editor of The London (Ontario) News.

William M. Davidson came to Calgary in December 1901. He founded The Morning Albertan and was the Editor-in-Chief for the next twenty-five years. However, he sold it to George M. Bell in 1926. Davidson also served two terms on the Calgary Public School Board.

He married twice. His first wife was Christina Robertson, daughter of Dr. James Robertson of Toronto, Superintendent of the Presbyterian Missions in Western Canada, who died in 1913. His second wife was Ethel Haydon, daughter of George Haydon, Publisher of the St. Thomas newspaper.

A prominent Liberal, Davidson was on the Calgary Liberal Association for many years., Interested in provincial politics, he successfully contested Calgary North in 1917, defeating Conservative, Rev. S. Bacon Hillocks. He sat until defeated in the 1921 general election. However, Davidson was re-elected as an Independent in the January 1923 Calgary by-election, caused by the death of Bob "Eye-Opener" Edwards. McCartney defeated Liberal candidate Clinton J. Ford to win and sat until he resigned his seat in 1925. Davidson retired in 1926.

Turning to federal politics, Andrew W. Davidson, running as a Liberal unsuccessfully contested the Calgary East riding in the 1925 general election. He was defeated by Conservative winner Fred Davis.

In 1930, he retired from business and moved to Victoria, B.C.

Died March 23, 1943 at Victoria at the age of seventy.

DAY, Dr. Arthur Melville

Born March 14, 1886 in Leith, Ontario, son of Daniel Cameron

Day and Jane Wilson Buzza.

Educated at Owen Sound Collegiate Institute, Day attended the University of Toronto, graduating with a Medical degree in 1913.

Dr. Day came to Alberta in 1913 and settled in Consort. He became a prominent physician and surgeon for forty-three years. As well, he became a successful farmer and a well-known Alberta stockman.

Active in community affairs, he was a member both of the Shriners and the Oldfellows. Moreover, Day was also an ardent curler.

A life-long Liberal, Dr. Day unsuccessfully ran three times for the Legislature and once for a seat in the House of Commons. In the general elections of 1921, 1926 and 1930, he was the Liberal candidate for Coronation. On all three occasions Day was defeated by the U.F.A. candidate, George N. Johnston.

In 1953, Dr. Day contested the federal riding of Acadia. However, the incumbent Social Creditor Victor Quelch was returned.

In 1955 he was named the Alberta Director of the Bank of Canada. He held this position up until the time of his death.

Dr. Arthur Melville Day died December 15, 1956 in Consort at the age of seventy.

DECHENE, Joseph Miville

Born October 22, 1879 in Chambord, Quebec, son of Leon Miville Dechene and Maria Pelletier. His ancestors settled in New France in the 17th century. His cousin was Joseph-Bruno-Aime Miville Dechene, who was a federal member for Montmagny, Quebec from 1917 to 1925.

Educated at Roberval, Dechene attended the Seminaire de Quebec. He came to Alberta in 1910, and became a pioneer settler of the Bonnyville area. He further became a prominent Therien farmer and land agent in both Bonnyville and Therien. Later he became a stockbroker. While also active in community affairs, Dechene served as the Councilor of Bonnyville.

In 1910, Dechene married Maria Gariepy, daughter of Joseph H. Gariepy. By marriage he was related to Senator Jean Leon Cote, Senator Prosper-Edmond Lessard, and Wilfrid Gariepy, a one-time

Alberta Cabinet Minister.

A Liberal, Joseph M. Dechene successfully contested Beaver River in 1921, defeating H. Montambault, the U.F.A. candidate, by a mere 617 votes. In his victory, he replaced Wilfrid Gariepy, who had returned to Quebec. Dechene sat in the Legislature for Beaver River until 1926, when he lost approximately half of his votes from his previous election and was defeated by John Delisle, the U.F.A. candidate. In 1930, he returned to the Legislature as the member for St. Paul and sat another five years on the opposition benches. Dechene was defeated in 1935 by Social Creditor, Joseph Beaudry.

Turning to federal politics, Dechene successfully contested the Athabasca riding in the 1940 war-time election, defeating an incumbent Member of Parliament, Percy John Rowe. Dechene sat in Parliament as the member of the large Northern Alberta riding for the next eighteen years. In the 1949 Canadian federal election, he defeated former MP Orvis A. Kennedy by a large margin. It was said that Joseph M. Dechene was the "smartest politician" that Alberta ever sent to Ottawa.

In the 1957 federal election, he retained his seat by a narrow 424 votes. However, he was not a candidate in 1958, retiring at the age of seventy-nine. He was a prominent Roman Catholic. His only son, Andre Dechene, became a Justice of the Alberta Supreme Court and later a Justice of the Alberta Court of Queen's Bench.

Joseph Dechene died December 1, 1962 in Edmonton at the age of eighty-three.

DESLISLE, John Amos

Born November 24, 1871 in North Hadley, Massachusetts, U.S.A., son of Peter Deslisle, a French Canadian by birth, and Leonna Wilford.

Deslisle came to Canada as a child with his parents in 1877 and was educated at country schools. In 1903, he founded the community of Deslisle, Saskatchewan, which was named in his honor.

He settled permanently at St. Paul, Alberta, where he became a successful farmer and an influential merchant.

John Amos Deslisle was returned as the U.F.A. member for the provincial Beaver River constituency in 1926. He sat in the Legislature for four years as a private member on the government side of the Chamber. In 1930, Deslisle was defeated by Liberal, Captain H.H. Dakin, by one vote after an official recount. He unsuccessfully attempted to re-enter the Legislature in 1935. In a field of four candidates, he came in third in an election that saw Social Creditor, Lucien Maynard, returned as the member for Beaver River.

DOUGLAS, James McCrie

Born February 5, 1867 in Middleville, Lanark County, Ontario, son of Rev. James Douglas, a Presbyterian minister, and Margaret Blyth. He came of pioneer stock.

Educated in Port Perry and after 1878 in Winnipeg, he then worked at Morris, Manitoba for sixteen years in the mercantile business. On November 1, 1894, he married Mary Cameron Bickerton.

Douglas came to the District of Alberta, N.W.T. in 1894. He settled in Strathcona where both him and his brother Robert Blyth Douglas, became prominent merchants. In this role, they were proprietors of a department store.

Active in community affairs, he served for two years on the Strathcona Town Council. Later after the amalgamation of Strathcona and Edmonton, Douglas served for four years as an alderman. In 1929 he was elected Mayor of the city for two years.

Interested in federal politics, James McCrie Douglas, running as a Liberal, successfully contested the 1909 Strathcona riding by-election, caused by the death of the sitting member, Dr. Wilbert McIntyre. He was elected by acclamation and then re-elected in 1911.

Douglas sat in Parliament for twelve years as a private member. In 1917, he broke with the Liberals over the conscription issue and was re-elected as a Borden government candidate.

In the December 1921 federal election, Douglas, running as a Conservative was defeated by D.W. Warner, the U.F.A. candidate by a 4,394 vote margin.

In June 1932, J.M. Douglas was appointed Stipendiary Magistrate for the Northwest Territories. He held power likened to that of a Supreme Court judge in civil and criminal cases, within the boundary of his jurisdiction. His appointment was made following the retirement of Judge Dubue who formerly administered the legal affairs of the Territories. He held this appointment for four years. In 1941, Douglas was re-elected an Edmonton alderman, and only retired from public life eight years later. Douglas was re-elected again in 1943, finishing first out of twelve candidates and in 1945, finishing first out of eleven candidates.

James Douglas died in Edmonton on March 16, 1950 due to a seizure. He was eighty-three.

DOZE, Isaac Stanley

Although born in Iowa, U.S.A., Doze came to the District of Alberta, N.W.T. in 1886 with his father Gus Doze, who homesteaded near Pakan, south of Smoky Lake. Educated in Pakan, he then helped in the operation of the family farm.

In 1907, Doze was appointed a homestead inspector by the federal government. He held this post for the next twenty-four years. Prime Minister R.B. Bennett's administration replaced him in 1931.

In January, 1932, Isaac Stanley Doze was one of the right Liberals whose names appeared before a nomination convention. This convention was used to select a candidate for the upcoming by-election for the federal riding of Athabasca, caused by the death of the sitting Liberal member G.F. Buckley. The other candidates included Joseph Dechene, M.L.A. for Beaver River, Frank R. Falconer, M.L.A. for Athabasca, E.E. Cross of Smoky Lake, Andrew Shandro, former M.L.A., H.H. Hiron, ex-Mayor of St. Paul, J. Mae Namara of Boyle, and H. Milton Martin of Edmonton. In the end, all but Martin declined to stand.

In the March 21, 1932 federal by-election, Doze placed second in the four-way contest in which he trailed Conservative lawyer Percy G. Davies by 324 votes. Doze amassed 4,586 votes whereas Davis amassed 4,910.

EAST, James

Born October 7, 1871 in Bolton, Ontario. While also educated in Bolton, East was forced to leave school at the age of thirteen to go and work in a wool mill. He then served his apprenticeship as a blacksmith.

In the 1890s East became a prospector in the Black Hills of South Dakota, New Mexico and Colorado. He travelled widely, taking part in the Australian Gold Rush.

In 1907 East came to Alberta and settled in Edmonton. Four years later he was sent to the Yukon to report on the Waugh claims at the junction of the Wind and Peel rivers.

Interested in the Labor Movement, East was first elected an Edmonton alderman in 1912, finishing fifth out of eighteen candidates.

During World War I, he enlisted in the Canadian Army with the Canadian Expeditionary Force, serving on hospital ships throughout the Atlantic. However, East was demobilized in 1919 and was re-elected to the city council. He served a total of 17 years on council.

Interested in federal politics, James East unsuccessfully contested the riding of Edmonton West in 1925, placing third in a field of three candidates. The former Liberal Premier, Charles Stewart, won the seat.

Turning to provincial politics, East unsuccessfully contested the multi-member Edmonton constituency in 1935. A year later, East joined the newly formed United People's League.

James East died June 23, 1940 at the age of sixty-eight and was survived by his wife and son.

ENZENAUER, Peter

Born in 1878 in Illinois. Enzenauer received a grade four education, before commencing to work for his living. Enzenauer's parents came from Germany.

He came to the District of Alberta, N.W.T. in 1904, and became an inventive and progressive Vulcan farmer. Utilizing innovative methods, Enzenauer was the only farmer in the district to use oxen to plough and pull wagons. He had twelve pairs of oxen to accomplish his desired tasks. Enzenauer further invented machinery to improve the harvesting of grain. In 1921 he sold his farm and purchased another one near Kitscoty.

Peter Enzenauer was an active member of the United Farmers of Alberta. He was returned as the member for the provincial Alexandra constituency in 1921 and was part of the 7th Alberta Legislative Assembly. He sat in the Legislature for 14 years as a private member on the government side of the chamber. In 1935 he was defeated by Social Creditor Selmer A. Berg. He then retired from politics and returned to his farm. Enzenauer later resided in Lloydminster and died in 1973.

EVANS, John P.

Born near Liverpool, England of Welsh parents. Evans was also educated in England.

He came to the District of Alberta, N.W.T. in 1903, and engaged in the lumber business. He became the Manager of the Crown Lumber Company at Athabasca. When the community went bankrupt, Evans was named the Commissioner. He later served as Secretary of the Athabasca municipality.

John P. Evans unsuccessfully ran as the U.F.A. candidate for the provincial Athabasca constituency in 1926.

FARQUHARSON, William George

Born April 23, 1888 in Walton, Ontario, son of David Farquharson, a native of Scotland. Educated in Brussels, Farquharson attended Seaforth Collegiate Institute where he qualified as a pharmacist. He practiced Pharmacy in Ontario for seven years.

Farquharson came to Alberta in 1912 and homesteaded in the Provost district, where he became a well-known farmer.

He was also a prominent member of the U.F.A. William George Farquharson was returned as the U.F.A. member for the provincial Ribstone constituency in the July 10, 1922 by-election, following the death of C.O.F. Wright. Farquharson amassed 1,596 votes, compared to the 408 votes won by second place Liberal candidate J.J McKenna. Farquharson sat in the Legislature for 13 years as a private member on the government side of the chamber. He is remembered today for his work as the Chairman of the Electoral

Redistribution Committee prior to the 1930 general election. In the 1935 Alberta election, he placed third and forfeited his deposit.

FEDUN, William Philip

Born August 23, 1879 in Zarydche, district Radekhiv, Galicia, in Austrian-occupied Poland, son of Pylyp (Philip) Fedun and Anna Fedun. He was also educated in Zarydche.

William Fedun came to the District of Alberta, N.W.T. in 1889 with his parents. The Fedun family homesteaded near Mundare. In 1902, William P. Fedun married Malania Wituk and they had two sons and two daughters. He became a well-known Krakow farmer who had not yet mastered the English language. Furthermore, he was a horticulturist of note.

William P. Fedun was returned as the U.F.A. member for the provincial Victoria constituency in 1921 where he defeated longtime Liberal incumbent Francis Walker. He sat in the Legislature for five years as a private member on the government side of the chamber. However, there is no record of him ever giving a speech. In the 1926 Alberta election, he did not seek re-election and retired from politics at the age of forty-seven.

Later he became a retail merchant, serving as a town Councilor. Fedun died November 14, 1949 in Krakow, Alberta.

FIELD, Jean Hunter

Born in 1872, Jean Hunter John married J.W. Field, a lumber merchant. Her husband was a Coal Branch mine manager for many years.

A northern Alberta pioneer, she became a resident of the Spurfield district in 1916. Mrs. Field was active in the U.F.A. movement for many years. She served as Vice-President of the United Farmers' Women's Association from 1924 to 1928. Field also had first-hand knowledge of the health and educational problems of the pioneers.

In 1930, Mrs. Field was nominated as the U.F.A. government candidate for Grouard (if elected, it was said at the time, she would replace the aging Mrs. Parlby in Premier Brownlee's cabinet). However, she was defeated at the polls by the sitting Liberal member, L. Alcidas Giroux, by a 689 vote margin.

From 1930 to 1936, Mrs. Field was an Edmonton Public School Trustee. Years later, Mrs. Field died on January 9, 1962 in Edmonton.

FIELDHOUSE, Henry Vernon

Born June 11, 1877 in Wooler, Ontario, son of Marmaduke H. Fieldhouse. His family moved to Manitoba when he was an infant.

Educated in Neepawa, Manitoba, Fieldhouse attended the Winnipeg Wesley College before entering the University of Manitoba, where he obtained a Law degree in 1900. He was admitted to the Bar and practiced for five years in Neepawa.

Fieldhouse came to Alberta in 1906. He practiced Law for two years in Vermillion before settling permanently in Wainwright, where he established himself as a prominent lawyer.

A staunch Liberal, H.V. Fieldhouse unsuccessfully contested the federal riding of Battle River in 1921. In a field of three candidates, he amassed 1,397 votes and placed third behind the winning U.F.A. candidate, Henry Spencer and Conservative, F.A. Morrison, who amassed 12,247 and 1,726 votes respectively.

FINN, Martin Francis

Born in 1884 in Massachusetts to Irish parents. Educated in his home state, Finn then worked for the Boston and Maine railway, in 1901. Later, he was an employee of the New York and New Haven railway system.

Martin Finn came to Canada in 1908 and joined the Canadian Pacific Railway in Winnipeg. The next year, he was transferred to Lethbridge, Alberta where he worked for the CPR for the next twenty years.

Active in the Trade Union Movement, he was a member of the B of RT organization from 1902 to 1913 when he joined the order of Railway Conductors. A year later, Finn was made Chief Conductor of the Lethbridge division. In 1916 he was appointed the representative to the CPR General Board for adjustment for the union. By 1921 he was

Chairman of all joint organizations of railway employees in the Lethbridge division.

Interested in federal politics, Martin F. Finn, running as the Labor Party candidate, amassed 3,170 votes, but unsuccessfully contested the Lethbridge riding in the 1921 general election. The seat was won by Lincoln H. Jelliff, the U.F.A. candidate, who won 4,961 votes.

During the campaign, Finn stated, "In the readjustment of things many antiquated ideas must be discarded. Usually fossils are found in the earth, but lately some have been discovered actually walking above ground. On Election Day, let us bury these fossils forever."

FORSTER, Gordon Alexander

Born April 30, 1884 in York, Ontario, son of John W. Forster and Mary Heard. His grandparents had lived in Muddy York in Upper Canada prior to the War of 1812. Educated in York, Forster attended the Ontario Agricultural College at Guelph.

Coming to Alberta in 1906, Gordon Forster and his brother, Hugh Forster, homesteaded in the Nateby district. They became well-known horse ranchers and farmers.

Active in the community, Forster was a Director of the U.F.A. Central Board from 1918 to 1921.

Gordon A. Forster was returned as the U.F.A. member for the provincial Hand Hulls constituency in 1921 as part of Alberta's 6th Legislative Assembly. He sat in the Legislature for fourteen years. However, he was not a candidate for re-election in 1935.

Gordon A. Forster died July 23, 1964 in Nateby.

FRAME, John W.

Born November 29, 1871 in Coatsbridge, Lanarkshire, Scotland. Frame came to Alberta in 1907 and first stayed in Edmonton. In 1912 he moved to Athabasca where he became a farmer.

John W. Frame was returned as the Liberal member for the provincial Athabasca constituency in 1926, taking 373 out of a possible 1,134 votes en route to defeating U.F.A. candidate J.P. Evans. He sat in the Legislature for four years as an opposition member. In 1930 he crossed the floor of the legislature and joined the United Farmers of Alberta. However, he unsuccessfully ran as their candidate for the provincial Athabasca constituency in 1930, losing by 196 votes. This situation of political opportunism misfired and a local merchant, Frank F. Falconer, held the constituency for the Liberals.

Frame died on December 8, 1932 at the age of sixty-one.

FULTON, William Rose

Born in the 1880s on a farm near Chesterville, Ontario, son of Perry Fulton. After being educated in Chesterville, Fulton then commenced farming with his father and brother.

Moving to Alberta in 1911, William Fulton settled in Rosedale, near Drumheller where he operated a store. In 1915 he moved to Drumheller where he was the proprietor of a men's clothing store. Throughout these endeavors, he became a well-known businessman.

Active in civic affairs, Fulton served a term as Mayor of Drumheller in 1918. He was in office when 8 people died of the Spanish Flu. Thus, plans for a municipal hospital were approved while he was Mayor.

Interested in politics, W.R. Fulton unsuccessfully contested the Bow River in 1921, being defeated at the polls by E.G. Garland, the Progressive candidate by a 7,948 vote margin.

Fulton died in 1960 in Drumheller. He was in his seventies.

GAETZ, Raymond L.

Gaetz came to the District of Alberta, N.W.T. in 1884. He first homesteaded in the Red Deer district where he established a small trading post with his brother. They were the first white traders between Edmonton and Calgary. He became a prominent Red Deer businessman and served as the Mayor of Red Deer from 1901 to 1903.

Raymond L. Gaetz unsuccessfully ran as the U.F.A. candidate for the provincial Red Deer constituency in the November 16, 1931 by-election. He placed second, losing to Conservative W. Ernest

Payne.

(His brother-in-law was G.W. Smith, the U.F.A. member for Red Deer from 1921 to the time of his death in 1931.)

GALBRAITH, Daniel Harcourt

Born in 1878 in Orangeville, Ontario, son of Robert Galbraith and N. Narshaw. Dr. C.T. Galbraith of Calgary was his brother. Also educated in Orangeville, Daniel H. Galbraith attended the Ontario College of Agriculture at Gault. While a student, he was a prominent champion athlete.

Galbraith came to the District of Alberta, N.W.T. in 1903 and homesteaded in the Vulcan district, where he became a well-known Vulcan farmer for the next forty-two years.

Interested in federal politics, Daniel Harcourt Galbraith running as a Non-Partisan candidate unsuccessfully contested the federal riding of Bow River, in the 1917 general election. In a field of four candidates, he placed third. The seat was won by H.H. Halladay, the government candidate. During the campaign, Galbraith endorsed the following Non-Partisan League resolutions: conscription of wealth and all resources as well as men, denouncing profiteers, asking nationalization of all transportation, telephone and telegraph lines and steamship lines, payment of $100.00 a month to soldiers, government insurance for soldiers, assurances by the government of protection against mortgages and taxes of soldier's homes, nationalization of banking and credit systems, and also of all industries organized on a national scale where competition had about ceased to exist, extension of the public domain to include all coal mines, water powers and forests, a federal legislation act including the recall of the sitting Members of Parliament, equal and unrestricted suffrage for both men and women, abolition of official charity and in its place the enactment of a national compulsory insurance law covering accident, illness, old age, and health, free administration of justice, abolition of the Canadian Senate, and a graduated income tax law.

Daniel H. Galbraith was returned as the U.F.A. member for the provincial Nanton constituency in 1921, and served on Alberta's 5th

Legislative Committee. He sat as a private member of the Legislature for nine years.

Galbraith retired from politics in 1930 at the age of fifty-two. Three years later, after having lost his vision, he moved to Bowness. In 1954 Galbraith published a book of verse, entitled "Happy Thoughts." He died on October 23, 1968 in Calgary at the age of eighty-nine.

GARDINER, Robert

Born February 24, 1879 in Aberdeenshire, Scotland. Although educated in Scotland, Gardiner came to Canada in 1902. He first worked as a farmhand at Indian Head, Saskatchewan for four years before homesteading near Excel, Alberta. He became a prominent farmer, engaged in wheat raising and horse breeding. He never married.

Active in community affairs, Gardiner was a founding member of the United Farmers of Alberta in 1909, and was reeve of the Golden Centre Municipal district for seven years.

Interested in federal politics, Robert Gardiner, running as a Progressive candidate, successfully contested the June 27, 1921 Medicine Hat by-election by defeating Col. Nelson Spencer by 9,764 votes. Gardiner was the first Progressive to enter the House of Commons. He was re-elected in the federal general election held the same year. Gardiner was also elected the Progressive (U.F.A.) member for the Acadia riding in 1925, 1926 and again in 1930 by acclamation. He sat in the House of Commons for 14 years. His determined stand with regard to the Beauharois Power Corporation affair resulted in the appointment of a special Committee of Inquiry by the House of Commons precipitating the Beauharois scandal. In 1931 on the retirement of the U.F.A. President Henry Wise Wood, Gardiner was selected as his successor.

In the 1935 federal election, Gardiner was defeated by Social Creditor Victor Quelch and retired from politics at the age of fifty-six. Gardiner was a member of the radical MP "Ginger Group" in the 1920s and 1930s. He died February 6, 1945 in Calgary at the age of sixty-nine. He was a Presbyterian.

GARLAND, Edward Joseph

Born March 16, 1886 in Dublin, Ireland, son of Dr. John Peter Garland and Mary Martin. Educated at Belvedere College, Garland attended Trinity College, Dublin University for two years. He was a Senior Sophistic at the time he left for Canada.

Garland worked for a year in Quebec and Ontario before coming to Alberta in 1910. He homesteaded in the Rumsey district, northeast of Calgary and became a prominent farmer. In 1916 Garland married Alfrieda Williams of Duluth, Minnesota. They had two sons: David Patrick Garland and John Edward Garland. He was a prominent Roman Catholic.

Active in the formation of the United Farmers of Alberta movement in 1909, Garland served on the Executive for a number of years. He was also active in community affairs, serving as Secretary-Treasurer of Muson-Big Valley District Association.

Edward J. Garland was returned as the federal Progressive (U.F.A.) member for the federal Bow River riding in 1921. He sat in Parliament for fourteen years as a private member on the opposition benches, being re-elected in 1925, 1926 and 1930. He was a prominent member of the so-called "Ginger Group" of Alberta Progressive members of Parliament that could make or break governments in the mid-1920s. However, in 1935, Garland was defeated by Social Creditor C.E. Johnston.

In 1932, Edward Garland founded the nationally organized C.C.F. party, based in Calgary. Three years later, he joined the Canadian Diplomatic Corps and was posted as the Secretary of the High Commissioner to Ireland. On May 4, 1946, Garland was named acting High Commissioner to Ireland and served until March 19, 1947. The next year, he was appointed Charge d'Affaires for Canada to Denmark. Furthermore, he was named the Ambassador to Norway on August 25, 1947 and to Iceland on March 16, 1949 with both posts ending on August 15, 1952. In 1953, he retired and moved to Creston, B.C.

Garland died in 1974 in Creston, B.C. at the age of eighty-six.

(See: The Canadian Who's Who 1936-1937)

GAUVREAU, Charles H.

A long-time pioneer resident of St. Paul, he was listed in the Henderson Directory in 1914 as a clerk. By 1920, Gauvreau was the agent for the United Grain Growers.

Interested in federal politics, Charles H. Gauvreau, running as a Conservative, unsuccessfully contested the newly created large northern riding of Athabasca in the 1925 general election. In a field of three candidates, he placed last. The seat was won by C.W. Cross, a prominent Liberal.

(By 1928, the only Gauvreau in St. Paul was Blanche Gauvreau who operated a general store. She was possibly Charles' widow.)

GERSHAW, Dr. Frederick William

Born April 11, 1883 in Emerson, Manitoba, son of Theodore Gershaw and Margaret Clark. Gershaw was also educated in Emerson, attending the University of Manitoba and graduating in Medicine.

Dr. Gershaw came to Alberta in 1906. He settled in Medicine Hat where he became a prominent physician and surgeon for the next forty years. Upon coming to Alberta, Gershaw worked for the Canadian Pacific Railway as a doctor. In 1912, he married Harriet Robinson, a registered nurse. They had four daughters: Margaret, Norma, Edith and Lorraine.

Active in community affairs, Gershaw served for twelve years on the Medicine Hat School Board.

Interested in federal politics, Dr. Frederick William Gershaw, running as a Liberal, unsuccessfully contested the Medicine Hat riding in the December 1921 general election. He was defeated by U.F.A. incumbent Robert Gardiner who had won the June 1921 federal by-election.

In the 1925 federal election, Dr. Gershaw was elected and held the seat for the next twenty years, except for the 1935 to 1940 period when it was held by the Social Credit.

In April 1945, Gershaw resigned his seat in the Commons on being appointed to the Senate by Prime Minister McKenzie King.

While in the Red Chamber, he was a prominent member of the Divorce Committee (At that time, the Senate had the power to grant divorces). He resigned in 1968.

Dr. Gershaw died June 26, 1968 in Ottawa at the age of eighty-five. Senator Gershaw School in Bow Island, Alberta is named in his honor.

GHASTLEY, Dr. Raymond C.

Born December 31, 1881 in Rogers, Minnesota, U.S.A., the son of a farmer. Also educated in Rogers, Ghastley attended the Los Angeles College of Osteopathic Physicians and Surgeons, graduating in 1909. He then practiced in Spokane, Washington for two years.

Dr. Ghastley came to Alberta in 1911 and settled in Edmonton, where he established an osteopathic practice. When anti-osteopathic legislation was proposed in the Legislature, Dr. Ghastley, with the aid of R.B. Bennett and J.K. Cornwall, two sitting members, was able to block its passage.

Interested in politics, Dr. R.C. Ghastley became active in the Social Credit Movement. In 1935, Aberhart passed him over and nominated Dr. W.S. Hall as the "official" Social Credit candidate for the federal riding of Edmonton East. Despite this, Dr. Ghostley contested the election as a Social Credit candidate. However, in a field of six candidates, he placed sixth while Dr. Hall was elected.

Subsequently Ghastley also contested seats on the Edmonton City Council without success. In campaigning for the election, as alderman, he urged the need of issuing community "scrip" and taxing of bonds in order to improve the city's financial position. He was a leading advocate of monetary reform.

Dr. Raymond Ghastley died in 1953 in El Reno, Oklahoma at the age of seventy-one.

GILLIS, Joseph E.

Born February 23, 1881 in Prince Edward Island, son of Stephen Gillis and Catherine McNeil. Educated in his home province, Gillis attended normal school, qualifying as a teacher. He taught school for five years until 1905 and then attended St. Dunston's University, Charlottetown, graduating in Arts.

Joseph Gillis came to Alberta in 1908 and settled in Macleod. He read Law under J.A. Matheson for five years and in 1913, he was admitted to the Alberta Bar. Gillis proceeded to establish a law practice in Blairmore, (in the Crowsnest Pass) where he was a prominent lawyer for the next twenty-four years. For many years he was in partnership with Donald G. MacKenzie.

Active in community affairs, Gillis also served on the town council and was a member of the school board for a number of years.

A Liberal, Joseph E. Gillis unsuccessfully contested the Macleod riding in the 1921 federal election. The seat was won by George G. Coote, the U.F.A. candidate.

Gillis died in 1937 in Blairmore at the age of fifty-six.

GORDON, Charles

Born April 13, 1877 in Ontario, son of Peter Gordon and Catherine McEwen. His father was a successful farmer. Gordon had three children: Anita, Douglas and Lorne.

Although Gordon was educated in Ontario, he moved to the District of Alberta, N.W.T. in 1903 and settled in Fort Saskatchewan where he worked as a carpenter. On November 25, 1905 Charles Gordon was one of the first citizens of Vegreville. A prominent businessman, he was in the lumber business for forty years. Notably, he built two of the early hotels in the community.

Active in community affairs, Gordon was a member of the first town council – a position he held for 15 years. He then was elected Mayor of Vegreville.

A Liberal, Charles Gordon twice unsuccessfully contested the Vegreville riding: first in the 1925 federal election and again in the 1930 election. In 1925 he amassed 2,643 votes but lost to Progressive candidate Arthur Moren Boutillier who had received 5,103 votes. In 1930 he amassed 4,500 votes but lost to U.F.A. candidate Michael Luchkovich who amassed 5,510 votes.

Charles Gordon died in 1936 in Vegreville at the age of fifty-eight.

GORESKY, Isidore

Born November 12, 1902 in the Austro-Hungarian Empire's province of Bukowina, son of Basil Goresky and Victoria Eustafliewich. Goresky immigrated to Canada as a child with his parents and was educated in Winnipeg. Qualifying as a teacher, he taught in Manitoba for a few years before attending the University of Manitoba, graduating in Arts in 1926.

Goresky came to Alberta and taught in Smokey Lake while working on a Masters degree from the University of Alberta. He taught from 1926 to 1934.

Isidore Goresky was returned as the U.F.A. member for the provincial Whitford constituency in 1930. He sat in the Legislature for five years as a private member on the government side of the chamber.

In the late 1930s, he became the Principal of the Edmonton Ukrainian Institute.

Goresky died February 22, 1999.

GRAHAM, Dr. Dawson

Born February 1869, in Oxford Station, Ontario, son of George Graham, a former Irish-born Presbyterian minister and Dorothy Lamrock. His father was an official with the CPR for many years.

Graham was educated at Belleville's Alberta College. He pursued further academic endeavors, attending Queen's University and graduating in Medicine in 1902. Dr. Graham then established a medical practice in Elm Creek, Manitoba before enrolling in the University of Manitoba Medical School. He obtained a Master's degree in 1906.

Dawson Graham came to Alberta in 1916. He practiced medicine for six years in Stettler before moving to Drumheller, where he remained for the next twenty years, becoming a prominent member of the community.

An active Conservative, Dr. Graham unsuccessfully contested the federal riding of Bow River in 1930, being defeated by J.E.

Garland, the incumbent U.F.A. member. J.E. Garland had amassed 5,825 voted compared to Graham's 4,653 votes.

GREENFIELD, Herbert

Born November 25, 1869 in Winchester, England, son of John Greenfield. Greenfield was educated at the Wesleyan School in Dalston. One of a large family, he halted his education to go to work for a grain shopping firm in London and carried on studies of economics and trade on his own time. In 1892, he came to Canada and worked on a farm in Ontario for the wage of $15 a month.

Greenfield came to Alberta in 1906 and homesteaded in the Westlock district, north of Edmonton. He was forty-one years of age at the time. A participant in co-operatives in the United Kingdom and a successful farmer in Alberta, Greenfield was an active member within the United Farmers of Alberta, later becoming their Vice-President.

Following the victory of the U.F.A. in the provincial election of 1921, Herbert Greenfield was chosen Premier only after Henry Wise Wood had declined and John Brownlee was passed over because he was a lawyer. He was a compromise candidate and proved to be unsuccessful as a provincial leader. He showed a lack of attention to public affairs, which involved the government in considerable criticism and caused the Liberal opposition to assert that the people had lost faith in the administrative ability of the ruling government. Distrust of Greenfield and opposition leadership increased when he sponsored a resolution in favor of greater immigration. This was diametrically opposed to a resolution on the same subject adopted by the U.F.A. convention. In November 1925, the long-expected resignation of Greenfield was announced and the elevation of Attorney General Brownlee to the premiership manifested.

However, Greenfield remained active in politics. He sat as a private member for a year, but was not a candidate for re-election in the 1926 general election.

On February 28, 1900, he married Elizabeth Harris, daughter of Samuel Harris of Adelaide Township, Ontario. They had two children: Franklin Harris and Arnold Leake. Herbert Greenfield then married Marjorie Parker Cormack upon the death of Elizabeth Harris in 1922.

In 1927, he was named Agent General for Alberta in London, a post he held for four years. On his return to Alberta, Greenfield was associated with the petroleum industry. He was President and Managing Director of Calmont Oil at the time of his death, which occurred August 23, 1949 in Calgary.

GRISDALE, Frank Sydney

Born July 8, 1887 in St. Marthe, Quebec, son of Albert B.G. Grisdale and Elizabeth Simpson. Grisdale attended Ste. Anne de Bellevue's MacDonald College, graduating with a Science degree in 1911.

Coming to Alberta, Grisdale became the Principal of Olds Agricultural College; a position he held for 17 years. Moreover, he was also a farmer. Frank S. Grisdale was returned as the U.F.A. member for the provincial Olds constituency in 1930, defeating Liberal George Clark. He sat in the Legislature for five years. In 1934 Premier Brownlee appointed Grisdale the Minister of Agriculture. Premier Reid reappointed him in July 1934. However, Grisdale was defeated in the 1935 general election by Social Credit Herbert Ash. In the 1940 Alberta general election, Grisdale ran unsuccessfully in a tight contest, losing to Social Credit candidate Norman Cook.

Frank S. Grisdale died in 1976.

HAYHURST, William

Born December 31, 1887 in Lyvennet Mill, Morland, England, son of Golbert Hayhurst and Sarah Burrows. Hayhurst was educated at Appleby Grammar School.

Coming to Alberta in 1910, William Hayhurst settled in Edmonton where he attended the University of Alberta. He then attended normal school, qualifying as a teacher. Hayhurst joined the staff at the Vegreville High School and a couple of years later was appointed the Principal. Active in community affairs, he also served as reeve of Minburn.

Interested in federal politics, William Hayhurst, running as a

Liberal, unsuccessfully contested the Vegreville riding in the 1930 general election. He was defeated by incumbent William Irvine. Hayhurst then switched parties, joining the Social Credit Movement in the mid-1930s. In the 1936 general election, Hayhurst was elected as the Social Credit member for Vegreville, defeating the U.F.A. incumbent, Michael Luchkovich by a 496 vote margin. Hayhurst sat in Parliament for five years and was succeeded in 1940 by Anthony Hlynka. In the 1940 Canadian federal election, Hayhurst ran as a New Democrat against incumbent Percy John Rowe and Liberal Joseph Miville Dechene, eventually losing to Dechene.

HENNIG, Rudolph

Born May 4, 1886 in Kirschnoff, Russia, son of Jacob and Katherine Hennig. Rudolph Hennig came to Western Canada in 1890 and farmed near Dunsmore during two years of drought, before permanently settling near Fort Saskatchewan. Educated in Josephburg, Hennig then assisted in the operation of the family farm. In time, Hennig became one of the most prominent farmers in the province. In 1909 he married Karoline Manz. They had two daughters and a son.

Active in community affairs, Hennig served forty-seven years on the school board. Notably, he was the President of the Alberta School Trustee's Association for eight years.

Rudolph Hennig was returned as the U.F.A. member for the provincial Victoria constituency in 1926 and for the newly created Clover Bar Legislature constituency in 1930. In 1930 he defeated Independent candidate Christian Hein. Hennig sat in the Legislature for nine years as a private member on the government side of the House. However, he did not seek re-election in 1935, retiring from politics at the age of forty nine.

In 1965, Rudolph Hennig was awarded an honorary Doctor of Laws degree from the University of Alberta. He died February 28, 1969 in Fort Saskatchewan at the age of eighty-two.

HERRON, John

Born November 15, 1953 in Ashton, Carleton County, Canada West, son of John Herron and Margaret Cram. Herron was also educated in his home town of Ashton.

In 1874, Herron enlisted as one of the original members of the North West Mounted Police. He came to the Northwest Territories with the force during the summer and helped establish Fort Macleod.

In 1877 Herron was present at the historic signing of the Treaty No. 7 at Blackfoot Crossing between the Canadian authorities and the Chiefs of the Storys , Cresams, Bloods, Sarcees and Blackfoot.

In 1878, he quit the force and lived in Ottawa for three years. During this time, Herron went into business. He also helped to organize the Princess Louise Dragoon Guards (a Militia Unit).

Returning to the District of Alberta, N.W.T. in 1881, John Herron, in partnership with a fellow officer of the Dragoon Guards, Captain Jack Stewart, established the Stewart Ranch near Pincher Creek. They stocked the ranch by bringing in 3,000 head of cattle and 1,000 horses that they had purchased in Utah. As a result, Herron became one of the most prominent Southern Alberta ranchers and operated his ranch for the next fifty-five years.

During the Northwest Rebellion of 1885, Captain Herron commanded the third troop of the Rocky Mountain Rangers (a Militia Unit).

Interested in federal politics, John Herron, running as a Conservative, successfully contested the newly formed Macleod riding in 1904, defeating Malcolm McKenzie by less than 100 votes. He sat in Parliament for seven years as a representative of the important cattlemen interests of the western Prairies. In 1911, Herron was defeated at the polls by Liberal Dr. David Warnock in the famous Reciprocity election.

As an aged policeman, John Herron twice attempted to regain his old seat in Parliament: First in 1921 and again in 1926.

He died on August 20, 1936.

HOADLEY, George

Born May 16, 1866 in Wetheral Abbey near Carlisle, Cumberland, England, son of George Hoadley (1829-1875) and Ann

Richardson. His family had received land during the reign of Henry VIII in the 16th century. Educated at Carlisle Grammar School, he attended St. Bee's. Hoadley then worked in Liverpool for the mercantile firm of McFee and Sons.

Coming to the District of Alberta, N.W.T. in 1890, Hoadley became a well-known farmer and rancher of the Okotoks district. He unsuccessfully ran for the North West Territorial Legislative Assembly in the High River constituency in 1902, being defeated by Richard Wallace.

George Hoadley was returned as the Conservative member for the provincial Okotoks constituency in 1909, winning against M. McHardy. He sat in the Legislature for 26 years. In 1917, he became the Conservative Party leader and Leader of the Official Opposition. In 1921 he was returned as the U.F.A. member. That year, Premier Greenfield appointed him both the Minister of Agriculture as well as the Minister of Health.

George Hoadley died on December 14, 1955.

HOLDEN, James Bismark

Born October 4, 1876, son of James Holden, a blacksmith and Sarah Service. Coming to Western Canada in 1891 at the age of fifteen, Holden worked at various jobs for two years before engaging in the grain trade in Manitoba.

Coming to the District of Alberta, N.W.T. in 1898, he settled first south of Edmonton near Leduc for seven years before finally settling at Vegreville.

Holden became a prominent businessman and proprietor of a real estate firm and insurance business.

Active in community affairs, he served as Mayor of Vegreville from 1915 to 1919 and also was on the school board for 16 years.

Interested in provincial politics, James B. Holden was elected by accumulation as the Liberal member for Vermillion in the July 16, 1906 by-election. He was twenty-nine years of age at the time and became one of the youngest members of the Legislature, sitting as a private member in the House for seven years. In 1909, Holden was re-elected as the member of the newly formed Vegreville constituency.

However, he was not a candidate in the 1913 general election.

Turning to federal politics, Holden unsuccessfully contested the Victoria riding as a government candidate in the December 1917 wartime election. He was defeated by Laurier-Liberal W.H. "Nobby" White. This was the only seat in Alberta that did not return a Borden government supporter. By 1921, Holden was a Conservative and again unsuccessfully contested the Victoria riding in the federal general election. Fourteen years later, Holden unsuccessfully contested the Vegreville riding in the October 1936 federal election.

IRONSIDE, Cyril M.

Born in 1903 in London, England, son of Edmond Ironside. Ironside was educated at Roan School, Greenwich, which is close to St. Alphegis Church where General James Wolfe, the victor of the Battle of the Plains of Abraham, is buried.

Ironside came to Alberta as a young man in 1919 with his family. They settled in the Blackfolds district where Cyril Ironside eventually became a well-known farmer.

Interested in provincial politics, Cyril Ironside running as the U.F.A. candidate, twice unsuccessfully contested Lacombe: first in 1935 and again in 1940.

During World War II, he enlisted in the Canadian Army and saw active service in Europe.

Turning to federal politics, Cyril M. Ironside, running for the C.C.F., unsuccessfully contested the Red Deer riding the 1949 general election. In a field of four candidates, he placed last and forfeited his deposit. The seat was retained by Social Credit incumbent Frederick D. Shaw.

In 1972, Cyril M. Ironside was still residing in the Lacombe district.

IRVINE, William

Born April 19, 1885 in Gletness, Shetland Islands, Scotland, son of William Irvine, a crafter and Vera Pottinger.

Irvine came to Canada in 1908 at the urging of Rev. J.S.

Woodsworth, assisting in the missionary work of the Methodist Church and attending Winnipeg's Wesley College. He was the Presbyterian minister at Emo, Ontario, from 1913 to 1915. In 1914 he was acquitted in ecclesiastical courts of the charge of heresy.

In time, Irvine like his mentor Rev. J.S. Woodsworth, started to preach a gospel of Socialism. A prolific writer, he edited "The Nutcracker," the official publication of the Non Partisan League.

Irvine came to Alberta in 1915 and settled in Calgary where he was a Unitarian minister for four years and a socialist writer. He served as Editor of the Western Farmer, and in 1919 he became a Bently farmer.

Interested in provincial politics, Rev. William Irvine, running as a Labor candidate, unsuccessfully contested Calgary South in 1917. In a field of three candidates, he placed second, trailing conservative Dr. Thomas H. Blow by a 1,025 vote margin.

After the war, he homesteaded in the Bentley district while continuing his journalistic endeavors.

William Irvine was returned as the Labor member for the federal Calgary East riding in 1921, defeating Liberal incumbent Stanley G. Tobin by a 747 vote margin. He was defeated in 1925 but returned as the U.F.A. member for the federal Wetaskiwin riding in 1926. Irvine was re-elected in 1930 but defeated in 1935. Moving to British Columbia, he was returned as the C.C.F. member for the federal Cariboo riding in 1945. He spent a total of 17 years in the House of Commons and was a close associate of J.S. Woodsworth.

Irvine was also a member of the "Ginger Group" in the 1920s and 1930s. In 1933 Irvine had been one of the founders of the Co-operative Commonwealth Federation (CCF) and became the party's first President in Alberta.

In 1910 he married Adelia M. Little. They had five Children.
William Irvine died October 27, 1962 in Edmonton.

(See: Anthony Mardiros, William Irvine, 1979)

JACKMAN, William J.

Jackman came to the District of Alberta, N.W.T. in 1901,

homesteading south of Edmonton.

He became a Bremner farmer in the Clover Bar district. He also became an active member of the United Farmers of Alberta Movement.

Interested in politics, William J. Jackman unsuccessfully contested the federal riding of Victoria in 1911 as a Farmers' candidate. In a field of three candidates, he placed third. The seat was retained by Liberal incumbent W.H. "Nobby" White.

William J. Jackman unsuccessfully ran as the only U.F.A. candidate in the five-member provincial Edmonton constituency in 1921. In a field of 26 candidates, he placed sixth, only missing being elected by a couple of hundred votes. The Liberals captured all five seats. During the campaign, Jackman stated that he did not think it would be good policy for the farmers to link themselves up with any other organization, including the Labor Party.

In 1923 he became a Director of the Alberta Wheat Pool. In 1926 he was named a Vice- President under Henry Wise Wood of the newly formed Alberta Wheat Pool.

The next year, Jackman was appointed a representative in Argentina of the Central Selling Agency of the Alberta Wheat Pool. His ability to speak the Spanish language fluently made him an ideal representative in South America.

JAMIESON, Col. Frederick Charles

Born May 18, 1875 in Carleton Country, Ontario, son of James Jamieson a successful farmer and Mary Ann Craig.

Educated at Kemptville, he taught school for two years.

Came to the District of Alberta, N.W.T. as a young man in 1895, he homesteaded in the Lacombe district for two years. He then moved to Edmonton, where he commenced reading Law under the direction of A.C. Rutherford. He was called to the N.W.T. Bar in 1899. He then practiced his profession in the firm of Rutherford and Jamieson. His career was interrupted by the South African War and then the Great War. Col. Jamieson became one of the most prominent lawyers in the city of Edmonton. He was awarded a K.C. in 1919 and remained active in Law until retiring in 1962. In 1901, he married Ann B.C. Macleod, who was recognized as one of the most beautiful women in Edmonton for years.

Active in civic affairs, he served for six years as the solicitor for Strathcona and arranged the amalgamation with Edmonton in 1911.

During the Boer War, he enlisted with the Canadian Mounted Rifles, serving as a trooper on the Veldt for three years. In 1906, he was active in the formation of the 19th Alberta Dragoons (Militia Unit), and was commissioned as a Major. At the outbreak of World War I, the Dragoons were the first unit mobilized and Col. Jamieson was named the commanding officer. He saw active service on the Western Front. In 1916, he was recalled and put in charge of the British Recruiting Mission in Chicago and later New York. In 1918, he was ordered to organize the 260th Canadian Rifles, which he commanded during the Siberian Campaign.

A staunch Conservative, Col. Jamieson contested successfully the 1931 Edmonton by-election, defeating Labor candidate, Elmer Roper by 2400 votes. He sat in the Legislature for one term. He failed in his re-election bid in 1935. In 1940, he contested unsuccessfully the federal riding of Edmonton West. On both occasions, the seat was retained by Liberal Cabinet Minister and former Premier, Charles A. Stewart.

JELLIFF, Lincoln Henry

Born April 26, 1865 at Oneida, Illinois, son of Fletcher Gould Jelliff and Mary White Wilcox. His grandfather Jerimiah Jelliff was a New England ship captain who was lost at sea. His ancestors had come to New England in colonial times from Stratford-on-Avon. The original spelling of his surname was Jolliffe and he was a distant relation of Lord Byng of Vimy Ridge.

Educated at Oneida, he attended Knox College, Galesburg, graduating with a Master's degree. He then read Law and was admitted to the Illinois Bar. He worked in the life insurance business for more than 13 years while taking his legal studies and education.

Jelliff practiced the legal professions for a number of years in the States. In 1894 he married Jennie P. Johnston of Obertin, Ohio. They were childless.

He came to the District of Alberta, N.W.T. in 1903, and homesteaded in the Raley district near Lethbridge. He became a prominent wheat farmer. Active in farm organizations, he was a Director of the Alberta Farmers Association, one of the roots of the United Farmers of Alberta Movement. He also advocated the extension of railway lines and lower freight rates in Southern Alberta.

Lincoln H. Jelliff was returned as the Progressive (U.F.A.) member for the federal Lethbridge riding in 1921. He sat in Parliament for nine years as a private member on the opposition benches. His legal training and experience helped him in his parliamentary duties. In 1930 he lost the U.F.A. nomination to Thomas O. King of Raymond and retired from politics at the age of sixty-five.

On April 16, 1945, he was living on his Raley farm at the age of eighty-one. He was a Congregationalist.

He died September 24, 1962 at the advanced age of ninety-seven.

JOHANSEN, John A.

Born in 1877 in Mount Pleasant, Utah of Danish American parents. Educated in his home-state, he taught school for a number of years.

He came to the District of Alberta, N.W.T. in 1904, and settled with his family on a farm near the new town of Raymond. Two years later, Johansen moved to Woolford where he became a well-known and outspoken farmer. Active in the U.F.A. Movement, he served on the local school board and was instrumental in the organization of the Cardston Municipal Hospital.

Interested in federal politics, John A. Johansen, running as the U.F.A-C.C.F. candidate, unsuccessfully contested the Lethbridge riding in the 1935 general election. In a field of 5 candidates, he placed fourth, and forfeited his deposit; Social Creditor John H. Blackmore won the seat. During the campaign, the Communist supported Johansen as a so-called "United Front" candidate. At the time, Tim Buck, the Communist National Leader, declared that his party supported Johansen as well as Arnold Webster, the C.C.F. candidate for Vancouver Burrard because of their stand on political issues.

JOHNSTON, George Norman

Born September 13, 1884 in Wingham, Ontario, son of William M. Johnston and Ellen Green. Educated at Wingham, Johnston attended London Collegiate Institute. He qualified as a teacher and taught near Listowel, Ontario for three years and then in Saskatchewan for another four years.

Active in the formation of the U.F.A., he was the President of Silverdale Co-operative Society for several years. Johnston was also a School Trustee.

George N. Johnston was returned as the member for the provincial Coronation constituency in 1921. He sat in the Legislature for the next fourteen years. In 1925, when Premier Greenfield resigned, his name was mentioned as a possible successor. John Brownlee became the Premier while Johnston was appointed the Speaker of the Legislature. He held this position for nine years. To the surprise of many, Johnston failed to win the U.F.A. nomination for Coronation prior to the 1935 general election. This was the first time in Alberta history that a Speaker suffered electoral defeat. He was defeated at the nominating convention and then retired from politics.

In 1940, Johnston came out of retirement to unsuccessfully contest the new constituency of Acadia-Coronation. He died September 28, 1977 at the age of ninety-three.

JOLY, Joseph Phymide "Laudas"

Born August 6, 1887 in St. Thomas D'Alfred, Quebec, son of Phymide Joly Corinee. According to "The Canadian Parliamentary Guide," his ancestors included Louis d'Aillehoust de Coulorge et D'Argenteny, who was the Governor of New France in the 1650s. Educated at St. Therese College, he attended Ottawa University.

Joly came to Alberta in 1908 and worked on a survey crew for seven years before he homesteaded in the St. Paul district. Laudas Joly became a well-known farmer and was active in the formation of the U.F.A. Movement.

J.P. Laudas Joly was returned as the member for the provincial St. Paul constituency in 1921. He sat in the Legislature for nine years. In 1930, Lessard's brother-in-law, Joseph M. Dechene, defeated him. He was also defeated at the polls in 1935.

J.P. Laudas Joly was returned as the Social Credit member for the provincial Bonnyville constituency in 1952. He sat in the Legislature for 12 years.

Joly died April 30, 1960.

KELLNER, Donald Ferdinand

Born September 15, 1879 in Ethel, Ontario, to Joseph Kellner and his Scotch wife Catherine Forsyth. Donald Kellner was educated at Listowel and was raised as a Presbyterian. He became an Edmonton district farmer.

Donald F. Kellner was returned as the U.F.A. member for the federal Edmonton East riding in 1921, defeating Joseph Clarke and incumbent Henry Arthur Mackie. He was defeated in his re-election bid in 1925 by former Alberta Liberal M.L.A. Charles Cross; Kellner was returned as the U.F.A. member for the federal Athabasca riding in 1926. He sat in the House of Commons for eight years. In 1930 he was defeated by Liberal John F. Buckley.

Kellner died April 1, 1935 in Edmonton.

KENNEDY, Donald MacBeth

Born August 21, 1884 in Haugh of Tullymet near Ballingburg, Perthshire, Scotland, son of Robert Kennedy and Margaret MacBeth. Educated at Perth Academy, Kennedy then came to Canada in 1903 to attend Brandon College, Manitoba, graduating in 1910. Donald Kennedy was raised as a Baptist.

Coming to Alberta in 1911, Kennedy became a Fairview, Peace River farmer, and served as a councilor for the Fairview municipal district and then as Secretary-Treasurer in 1917. He held this position for two years. In 1916, he married Mabel May Macdonald of Saskatoon. They had three daughters. He was active in the United Farmers of Alberta organization.

Donald M. Kennedy was returned as the U.F.A. member for the provincial Peace River constituency in July 1921. Kennedy defeated incumbent Liberal W.A. Rae and E.S. Farr. He vacated his seat so that Premier Herbert Greenfield could enter the Legislature in the subsequent by-election.

Donald M. Kennedy was then returned as the Progressive (U.F.A.) member for the federal Edmonton East riding in December 1921, which included the Peace River Country. He defeated former Alberta Liberal MP Frank Oliver and former Alberta Conservative M.L.A. Robert Campbell. He was a prominent member of the so-called "Ginger Group" of Alberta members. He sat in the House of Commons for 14 years, being re-elected for the newly formed Peace River riding in the 1925, 1926 and 1930 federal elections. In 1935, Social Creditor Rene Antoine Pelletier defeated him.

While in the Commons, he fought for the building of a rail link from the Peace River country to the Pacific coast. In the 1926 government crisis, Kennedy's vote was said at the time to have resulted in the toppling of Arthur Meighan's shadow Cabinet and the assuring that the Liberals would be asked to form a government.

He then retired from politics to his farm, spending his free time reading. Donald M. Kennedy died September 25, 1957.

KING, Thomas Owen

Born December 6, 1869 in Salt Lake City, the son of Thomas O. King and Dorcas Debenham, Utah pioneers. As a child, King's family moved to Cassia County, Idaho, where he was educated.

Coming to the District of Alberta, Northwest Territories in 1892, King worked first as a cowboy on the Pilling ranch and then as the foreman on the church-owned Cochrane ranch. In 1903, he settled at Raymond, in partnership with his brother, operating a general store for many years as well as farming. He was elected a Raymond School Trustee in 1908. With the exception of one year, he served as a School Trustee until 1937.

Thomas Owen King ran twice, unsuccessfully, in politics: first as a Conservative for the provincial Cardston constituency in 1917, and then again as the United Farmers of Alberta candidate for the federal Lethbridge riding in 1930. In 1917, incumbent Liberal Cabinet Minister J.J. McLean defeated him. In 1930, Conservative Dr. John Stewart defeated him. He aided in the establishment of the U.F.A. Movement and was also a respected member of the Church of Jesus Christ of Latter-day Saints.

In 1890 King married Margaret Helen Arbon. They had five daughters and three sons. He served as a Mormon missionary in England from 1906 to 1908. He died in 1946 in Raymond at seventy-seven years old.

LAKEMAN, Jan

Born in 1887 in the Netherlands.

As a youth, Lakeman was apprenticed to a carpenter and worked in this occupation all his life. While still young, he became an active and dedicated Communist. He was arrested for taking part in an anti-military organization and served four months in a Dutch prison as a result.

Lakeman came to Alberta in 1910, he settled in Edmonton where he was a part of influential labor circles for the next forty-five years.

Active in civic affairs, Lakeman ran several times for a seat on the Edmonton City Council but was never elected.

In 1922, Lakeman became one of the original members of the Communist Party of Canada and, after it became illegal, a member of the Labor Progressive Party in the 1940s and 1950s. He was the inaugural leader of the Alberta Communist Party.

Interested in both Albertan and Canadian politics, Jan Lakeman was unsuccessful in being elected to the Legislature on four occasions and sought election to the House of Commons three times.

In 1926,he ran both provincially and federally in Edmonton. Three years later, he attended the Pan-Pacific Trade Union Conference in Moscow.

On his return from the Soviet Union, he was expelled from the carpenters union and lost his job with the Canadian National Railway; he became active in the unemployment movement. In the provincial and federal elections in 1930, Lakeman ran again as a candidate of the

Labor Farmer Unity League, a pro-Communist organization. His percentage of votes gained was always less than ten percent. He contested the 1931 provincial Edmonton by-election and the 1935 Alberta general election.

In 1940, Lakeman was arrested under Section 29A of the Defence of Canada Regulations (War Measures Act) and was sent to an internment camp in Kananaskis. Other prominent Alberta Communists, including Calgary alderman Pat Lehinan, Ben Swankey, William Tiromi, William Repka and Alex Miller, were arrested at the same time and were sent to the same internment camp. Lakeman was released in September, 1942 and returned to Edmonton where he became active in the Labor Progressive (Communist) Party. In 1945, Lakeman unsuccessfully contested the Edmonton East riding. In a field of five candidates, he placed last and forfeited his deposit.

He died November 7, 1956 in Edmonton at the age of sixty-nine.

LEE, Raymond M.

Born in 1889, Lee attended the University of Alberta, graduating with a degree in Law.

He was admitted to the Alberta Bar in 1914.

Lee moved to Provost, Alberta, where he established a legal firm. He became a prominent lawyer for the next thirty-five years. He also operated a large farm. Active in community affairs, he served on the Provost Village Council and also served as a reeve of the municipal district. He was the Chairman of the Hospital Board for twenty-nine years.

Turning to federal politics, Raymond M. Lee, running as a Liberal, unsuccessfully contested the Battle River riding in the 1925 general election. In a field of three candidates, he placed second but forfeited his deposit. U.F.A. incumbent Henry E. Spencer retained the seat.

Lee died April 3, 1949 in Provost, at the age of sixty.

LEEDY, John Witnah

Born March 8, 1849 in Richland County, Ohio, Leedy's parents were members of the Dunkard Church. During the American Civil War, young Leedy tried to enlist at the age of fourteen in a company leaving for the front but was rejected. He remained with the company, however, until the end of the war. He then worked as a clerk in a store in Pierceton, Indiana for three years. In 1868, he worked on a farm at Carbinville, Illinois. Twelve years later, he moved to Kansas, where he became a prosperous farmer near Leroy, Coffey County.

In the 1880s Leedy married Sarah J. Boyd of Frederickstown, Ohio. They had a son, Boyd Leedy of Seattle, and two daughters.

Originally a Republican, Leedy became a Democrat in 1872, until the organization of the Populist Party, of which he became a leader. He was elected to the Kansas Senate in 1892. He sat until elected Governor of Kansas in 1896. He was Governor of Kansas for three years, being elected on a "populist" ticket. After suffering political defeat in 1899, he called a special session of the Kansas Legislature and passed several controversial pieces of legislation. In 1901, he moved to Alaska, where he became wealthy after discovering a gold mine. He served as Mayor of Valdez and practiced Law even though he had no formal legal training.

Coming to Alberta in 1908, John Leedy became a prosperous Whitecourt farmer. He was a friend of Henry Wise Wood and Donald M. Kennedy. He became active in the U.F.A. Movement.

In 1917, Leedy became the leader of the "Non-Partisan" League. Interested in provincial politics, he unsuccessfully contested Gleichen in 1917 as the League's candidate. In a field of three candidates, he placed last and forfeited his deposit. Two "Non-Partisan" candidates were elected: Mrs. McKinney in Claresholm and James Weird in Nanton.

Turning to federal politics, J.W. Leedy, running as an Independent, unsuccessfully contested the Victoria riding in the war-time 1917 general election. In a field of three, he placed last. However, it was said at the time, his 602 votes resulted in Laurier Liberal W.H. "Nobby" White defeating Unionist (government) candidate J.B. Holden by a narrow 523 vote margin. Victoria riding was the only one of Alberta's 12 ridings to elect an Opposition candidate.

His more radical views carried him away from the U.F.A. only a few months before the agrarian movement captured the Alberta Legislative Assembly in 1921. He advocated radical changes in the banking system.

Retiring from farming, the former Kansas Governor ran provincially for the last time when he was seventy-seven years of age: in 1926, Leedy unsuccessfully contested the five-member Edmonton constituency. In a field of eighteen candidates, he placed last and forfeited his deposit.

He died March 25, 1935 in Edmonton, at the age of eighty-six. He had been in failing health for several months. He was buried in Edmonton.

Leedy had lost all of his money in the Great Depression. His impoverishment came to Kansas Legislature's notice; which passed a special piece of legislation appropriating $1,000 to cover his funeral expenses and a grave marker. It says in part: "John W. Leedy, 13th Governor of Kansas, Sincere Purpose, Simple in Manner, Rugged in Speech, His Public Services are here commemorated by the People of Kansas."

LOVE, Rev. George A.

Reverend George A. Love was a Presbyterian minister.

Love became a Rosebud farmer. He served as the Mayor of the Town of Red Deer from 1903 to 1904.

Active in the U.F.A., he served on the Executive and was a long-time personal friend of Henry Wise Wood.

George A. Love unsuccessfully ran as the U.F.A. candidate for the provincial Bow Valley constituency in 1921. He placed second, losing to Liberal incumbent Charles R. Mitchell.

LOVE, John Russell

Born January 9, 1895 in Toronto, Ontario, to Harry W. Love and Ada Breckon. Russell Love moved with his parents to Edmonton when he was still a boy. He attended the University of Alberta, graduating in 1920. At the outbreak of World War I, he enlisted in the Canadian Army and served overseas. He then became a prominent farmer of the Irma district.

J. Russell Love was returned as the U.F.A. member for the provincial Wainwright constituency in 1921. He sat as a backbencher until 1934 when Premier Reid appointed him Provincial Treasurer. He was defeated in the 1935 general election and later represented producers in the Alberta Dairymen's Association and served several terms as President of the Alberta Co-operative Wholesale Association.

In 1925, he was married to Catherine McCrimmon.

J. Russell Love died February 9, 1985. He was a Protestant.

LOVERING, Dr. James Edward

Born November 5, 1871 in Coldwater, Ontario, son of John Lovering and Mary Lynch.

Educated in Coldwater, Lovering qualified as a school teacher. He then taught in Revelstoke, B.C. for twelve years. Returning to the East, he attended McGill University, graduating in Medicine in 1908.

Lovering came to Alberta in 1908 and settled in Magrath where he practiced Medicine for four years. In 1912, he moved to Lethbridge where he became a prominent physician and surgeon.

Active in community affairs, he served two years on the Lethbridge City Council. He was twice a candidate for the Mayoralty, the latter time in 1926 when he was defeated by W.D.L. Hardie by a mere 178 votes. On his first attempt, in 1921, he placed last, losing to Progressive candidate Lincoln Henry Jelliff. He also served fifteen years on the school board. An ardent pacifist, he was opposed to cadet training in the Lethbridge schools.

Dr. James E. Lovering, a Liberal, unsuccessfully contested the Lethbridge riding in 1926. In a field of four candidates, he placed last.

In the 1930s, he became an active Social Creditor. In 1935, he was on the S.C. short list as both the federal and provincial candidate for Lethbridge, but was not the party's final choice.

Died August 12, 1936 at Lethbridge at the age of sixty-four.

LUCAS, William Thomas

Born July 26, 1875 in Bailieboro, Ontario, son of John William

Lucas and Margaret Fair. Educated at Bailieboro. William Thomas Lucas attended the Ontario Agriculture College in Guelph. He then returned to Bailieboro to help run the family farm.

In 1906, Lucas moved to Toronto where he worked for two years before moving to Vancouver where he worked for ten years.

Coming to Alberta, Lucas became a well-known Lougheed farmer. In 1903, he married Charlotte Perrin. They had a son and two daughters. He became active in the United Farmers of Alberta Movement.

William T. Lucas was returned as the Progressive (U.F.A.) member for the federal Camrose riding in 1921. Lucas defeated the incumbent member W.H. "Nobby" White and Alberta M.L.A. James Bismark Holden by a 9,662 vote margin. He sat in the House of Commons for 14 years. In the 1925 federal election, he was re-elected to represent the newly- formed Camrose riding. In 1935, Social Creditor John A. Marshall defeated him. He was an active Freemason and an Anglican.

(In 1972, he was living in retirement in Peterborough, Ontario at the age of ninety-six.)

LUCHKOVICH, Michael

Born November 13, 1892 in Shamokin, Pennsylvania, U.S.A., son of Ephraim Luckovich. Both of Luchkovich's parents were of ethnic Ukranian descent.

Michael Luchkovich came to Canada in 1907 and attended the University of Manitoba, graduating with a degree in Arts. He then attended the University of Calgary where he majored in Political Science and earned his teaching qualifications at the Calgary Normal School. He became a school teacher in Vegreville, Alberta.

Michael Luchkovich was returned the U.F.A. member for the federal Vegreville riding in 1926. He sat in the House of Commons for nine years. In 1935, Social Creditor William Hayhurst defeated him.

Luchkovich was a Greek Catholic and a leader in the Edmonton Ukrainian Community.

Michael Luchkovich died April 21, 1973.

LUNNEY, Harry W.

Born January 20, 1885 in Saint John, New Brunswick, son of Thomas Lunney and Katherine Lanalum. Lunney was educated at the Saint John Public School and then attended the University of New Brunswick, graduating from the Arts program in 1906. He then studied at King's College, Windsor, Nova Scotia, obtaining a degree in Civil Law in 1908.

As a young man he was a newspaper reporter in Saint John and later a member of the editorial staff of The Montreal Star.

Lunney came to Alberta in 1911 where he joined the staff of The Calgary News Telegram. He also established a Calgary legal practice. Interested in federal politics, Harry Lunney, running as a Liberal, unsuccessfully contested the Calgary West riding in the 1926 general election. He was defeated by the Conservative lawyer and Prime Minister to be, R.B. Bennett by a 2,449-vote margin.

Justice Minister Ernest Lapointe appointed Lunney as a Justice of the Supreme Court, Appellate Division. He was only 43 at the time, the youngest in Canada. In 1908, he married Elma, daughter of Dr. M.C. Costello, a Mayor of Calgary.

Lunney was a Roman Catholic. Due to failing health, he resigned from the Bench in September 1944.

Lunney died December 23, 1944 in Calgary at the age of fifty-nine.

LYMBURN, John Farquhar,

Born September 20, 1880 in Ayr, Scotland, son of William Lymburn and Margaret Farquhar. Educated in Ayr, he attended Glasgow University, where he studied Law. He was admitted to the Scottish Bar in 1906. He then practiced Law in Glasgow and Hamilton for five years.

Coming to Alberta in 1911, Lymburn joined the Edmonton legal firm of Short and Cross. He practiced Law in the city for the next 56 years. In 1912, he married Isabella Marguerite Clark, daughter of a former Chief Constable of Hamilton. They had three daughters.

John Farquhar Lymburn was named to Premier John Brownlee's Cabinet as the Attorney General on June 5, 1926. He was returned as a U.F.A. member for the multi-member Edmonton constituency in the June 26, 1926 general election. He sat in the Legislature for nine years as the Attorney General until 1935, when he was defeated.

In the September 22, 1942 Edmonton by-election, Lymburn failed in his bid to re-enter the Legislature. This time he ran as an Independent.

John F. Lymburn died November 25, 1969. He was a Presbyterian.

(See: The Canadian Who's Who, 1967)

MacLACHLAN, George

Born February 3, 1881 in Glasgow, Scotland, son of John MacLachlan and Catherine McIntosh. George MacLachlan was educated in Glasgow.

George MacLachlan came to the District of Alberta, N.W.T. as a young man in 1900 and homesteaded near Clyde in the Pembina district. He served on the municipal council and the school board for a number of years.

MacLachlan was an active member of the United Farmers of Alberta Movement. He was returned as the member for the provincial Pembina constituency in 1921.

He sat in the Legislature for fourteen years as a government member. In 1935, he placed third to Dr. Harry Brown, the Social Credit candidate. In the 1940 Alberta election, MacLachlan was re-elected as Independent member for Pembina and sat one term in the Legislature. In 1944, he was again defeated and retired from politics at the age of sixty-three.

MacLachlan was a Presbyterian and was never married.

MacLELLAN, John James

Born in 1879 in Pictou County, Nova Scotia, John James

MacLellan was a fifth-generation Canadian of Scotch descent. John MacLellan trained to be a blacksmith. In 1905, he came west to Gladstone, Manitoba for the harvesting.

He came to Alberta in 1907 and settled in Taber where he worked as a blacksmith for two years before homesteading near Purple Springs. Active in community affairs, MacLellan served as the reeve of the municipal district of Eureka and was a prominent member of the United Farmers of Alberta. He was also a Director of United Grain Growers for twenty-five years.

John James MacLellan was returned as the member for the provincial Taber constituency in 1930. He sat in the Legislature for five years. In 1934, Premier Reid appointed MacLellan to the Cabinet as Minister of Public Works. He sat in the Legislature for five years, serving as Minister of Public Works for 1935-35. In 1935 Social Creditor James Hansen defeated him.

He retired from politics to his Purple Spring farm. It is said that MacLellan was the first Roman Catholic to be elected from rural southern Alberta.

In 1954, John James MacLellan retired from farming and moved to Lethbridge, where he died one year later in 1955. He was a Roman Catholic.

MARSHALL, Duncan Maclean

Born September 24, 1872 in Eldersile township, Ontario, son of John Marshall, a farmer, and Margaret McMurchy.

Marshall was educated at Walkerton School and Owen Sound Collegiate Institute. He taught school from 1890-1894, in rural Ontario before becoming a journalist. He worked for and owned several small town Ontario newspapers including The Brace-bridge Gazette. He was also an organizer of the Patrons of Industry Movement in Ontario.

Interested in federal politics, Duncan McLean Marshall, running as a Liberal, unsuccessfully contested the Muskoka (Ontario) riding in the 1904 general election. He was defeated by Conservative William Wright by a 486-vote margin.

Duncan came to Alberta in 1905 and he managed the Edmonton Daily Bulletin and owned the The Olds Gazette. Duncan further became a famous breeder of shorthorn cattle on his Olds ranch.

A Liberal, Duncan Marshall successfully contested Olds in 1909 and sat in the Legislature for twelve years. He held three portfolios in the Provincial Cabinet – Minister of Agriculture 1909-1921; Provincial Treasurer November 1909-May 1910; and Provincial Secretary November 1, 1909-May 26, 1910. After being defeated in Olds in July 1921, he entered federal politics. Duncan unsuccessfully contested the Calgary East riding in the December 1921 election. Marshall then returned to Ontario. In 1934, he successfully contested Peel and sat in the Ontario Legislature until he was defeated in 1947. Premier Hepburn appointed him Minister of Agriculture in 1934. He held this portfolio for four years. He was called to the Senate, January 20, 1938 by William Lyon MacKenzie King. He was author of Shorthorn Cattle in Canada.

Duncan died January 16, 1946 in Toronto, at the age of seventy-four. It was said that Marshall and R.B. Bennett were the best debaters in the Second Alberta Legislature.

MARSHALL, Robert Colin

Born May 19, 1883 in Ingersoll, Ontario, son of Peter Marshall and Katherine Allan.

Educated at Ingersoll.

Marshall came to the District of Alberta, N.W.T. in 1902 and settled in Calgary in 1906 where he entered the contracting business as Secretary-Treasurer of Crown Paving Company. He remained associated with this business for the next sixty years. During this time, Marshall became a prominent Calgary businessman.

Active in community affairs, he served as a city alderman for three years. In 1919, he was elected Mayor of Calgary. He held this position for two years, from January 2, 1919 to January 3, 1921. In his first year as mayor, he married Daisy Mary MacGregor, and together they had two children: Donald and Joan Marshall.

A life-long Liberal, Robert Colin Marshall successfully contested the multi-member Calgary constituency in the 1921 Alberta election. He was the only one of the five elected members that was a Liberal. He sat in the Legislature for five years. He failed in his bid to be re-elected in the 1926 election.

In 1928, he moved to Edmonton but remarried a partner of the Crown Paving Company. On two occasions, he served as President of the Alberta Northwest Chamber of Mines.

In 1937, on the death of Lt. Governor Philip Carteret Hill Primrose, Marshall's name was mentioned as a possible successor. However, he was passed over by Prime Minister MacKenzie King who named John C. Bowen.

Turning to Federal politics, R.C. Marshall unsuccessfully contested the March 21, 1938 Edmonton East by-election, caused by the death of Social Credit incumbent Dr. W.S. Hall. He was defeated by Social Creditor Orvin Kennedy.

In 1961, Marshall retired and sold his share of the Crown Paving Company.

February 20, 1962, while on holiday in Fort Lauderdale, Florida, Marshall died at the age of seventy-eight.

MATHESON, Archibald Malcolm

Born March 31, 1891 in Glenlivet, Banffshire, Scotland, son of Donald Matheson and Marjory MacKay. Matheson was of Scottish descent. Educated at Tomintoul, he attended Aberdeen University and the Aberdeen Commercial College.

Coming to Alberta in 1912, he joined the Canadian Bank of Commerce. Later he worked for Merchant's Bank of Canada for three years. Leaving the bank, Matheson became a prominent Mundare farmer and stock broker. He was an active member of the United Farmers of Alberta Movement.

Archibald M. Matheson was returned as the member for the provincial Vegreville constituency in 1921. He sat in the Legislature for 14 years. In 1935 he was defeated by Social Creditor Dr. James L. McPherson.

Matheson was an Anglican.

MATHESON, Joseph Duncan

Born February 8, 1873 in Malagawatch, Inverness County, Nova Scotia, son of Murdock Matheson. Matheson was educated at the Pictou Academy and then attended Dalhousie University, graduating with Honors in 1899. He articled with Daniel McLennan, K.C., in Port Hope, N.S. and was admitted to the Nova Scotia Bar the same year. He opened a law office in Port Hope where he practiced for the next 13 years.

Matheson came to Alberta in 1912 where he was admitted to the Alberta Bar in January 1913. He practiced Law with D.M. MacLiannon of Edmonton for four years.

In 1916, Matheson moved to Macleod where he practiced Law for the next sixteen years. He was named the Crown Prosecutor of the Macleod Judicial District in 1922. He was awarded a K.C.

Interested in federal politics, Joseph D. Matheson, running as a Conservative, unsuccessfully contested the Macleod riding in the 1930 general election. He was defeated by U.F.A. incumbent George G. Coote by a 792 vote margin.

Justice Minister Hugh Guthrie appointed Matheson Judge of the Peace River District Court in 1934. He succeeded the legendary Judge Dubuc. A year later, when the courts were reorganized, he was transferred to the Northern Alberta District Court.

Matheson retired from the Bench in 1948.

Joseph Duncan Matheson died November 2, 1967, in Macleod

at the advanced age of ninety-four.

McCALLUM, Joseph Seeley

Born July 9, 1884 in Renfrew, Ontario, son of McCallum and Jane Seeley.
McCallum came to the District of Alberta, N.W.T. in 1892 with his parents and his family settled at Beaver Lake.

Educated in Beaver Lake and Edmonton, he attended the Regina Normal School, qualifying as a teacher. He taught briefly in Fort Saskatchewan before homesteading in the Mundare district. Later he went into real estate and became a prominent Mundare stock dealer and implement agent.

Interested in provincial politics, Joseph Seeley McCallum successfully contested the Vegreville constituency as a Liberal in 1913, defeating Peter Savarich in the process. He sat in the Legislature for eight years. In 1921, he was defeated in his re-election bid by A.M. Matheson, the U.F.A. candidate.

Turning to federal politics, McCallum, running as a Liberal, unsuccessfully contested the Vegreville riding in the 1935 general election. In a field of five candidates, he placed third. Social Creditor – former Liberal – William Hayhurst, won the seat.

McCOOL, Robert Milton

Born August 30, 1893 in Pilot Mound, Manitoba, son of James McCool and Catherine L. McGee. McCool was of Scottish descent. Coming to the District of Alberta, N.W.T. as a child, his father homesteaded in Crossfield, near Calgary. Educated in Crossfield, he then went into partnership with his father. McCool became a well-known farmer.

Robert McCool became active in the United Farmers of Alberta Movement. In 1921, he was the campaign manager of the Cochrane U.F.A. member, Alex Moore. Moore was re-elected. In 1926, Moore failed to show up to sign his nomination papers due to an automobile accident, and so Robert M. McCool became the U.F.A. candidate.

McCool was returned as the member for the provincial

Cochrane constituency in the June 26, 1926 general election. He sat in the Legislature for nine years. In 1935 Social Creditor William R. King defeated him. He then retired from politics to his farm.

McCool was a Director of the Alberta Co-operative Wholesale Society and a life-insurance agent. He was a Presbyterian.

Robert Milton McCool died June 22, 1988.

McDANIEL, Hugh Campbell

Born in the 1880s in Bloomington, Illinois.

McDaniel was educated in Bloomington, and worked different jobs before moving to Cooperstown, North Dakota, where he was a clerk in a general store and played semi-professional baseball.

McDaniel came to Alberta in 1909, where he homesteaded in the Whitla district, near Medicine Hat. McDaniel became a well-known farmer. In 1912, McDaniel, in partnership with Harry Gray, purchased a team plowing and threshing outfit.

Interested and active in the United Farmers of Alberta Movement, he was selected the party's federal candidate for the Medicine Hat riding in 1925, defeating P.H. Webberburn of Redcliff and Carl Axelson of Bingville.

In the October 1925 federal election, Hugh Campbell McDaniel was defeated by Liberal Dr. Frederick W. Gershaw by a 1,986-vote margin.

In 1926, McDaniel moved to Whitla.

McGILLIVRAY, Alexander Andrew

Born February 12, 1884 in London, Ontario, son of Rev. Daniel McGillivray and Isabella Haggart. McGillivray was educated at St. Francis College in Richmond, Québec and then attended Dalhousie University, graduating with a degree in Law.

McGillivray came to Alberta in 1907. He was admitted to the N.W.T. Bar in May of that year before the Alberta Courts were organized. He started practicing Law in Stettler in 1908. However, two years later, he moved to Calgary where he became a prominent lawyer, creating a law firm with Thomas Tweedie. He was awarded a K.C. in

1919. A brilliant barrister, McGillivray drew up contracts which brought the Alberta Wheat Pool into existence. He was a Special Crown Prosecutor in the murder trial of Picarielle and Mrs. Lassandra. Both were convicted of killing an Alberta Provincial police officer.

An active Conservative, A.A. McGillivray unsuccessfully contested the Red Deer riding in the 1911 federal election. He was defeated by Liberal incumbent Dr. Michael "Red" Clark. At a 1925 Conservative Leadership Convention, McGillivray was elected the party's Alberta leader. McGillivray entered the Legislature when he headed the polls for the multi-member Calgary constituency in the 1926 provincial election. He served as the Conservative Alberta leader until 1929. He sat in the Legislature until 1930, but was not a candidate in the general election held that year.

Justice Minister Hugh Guthrie appointed him as a Justice of the Supreme Court, Appellate Division in 1931. McGillivray was 47 at the time, which made him one of the youngest Supreme Court Justices in the country.

Alexander Andrew McGillivray died December 12, 1940 of a heart attack in Edmonton, at the age of fifty-four. In 1911, he married Margaret Hall of Montreal. His only son is William A. McGillivray, who was the Chief Justice of Alberta from 1985 to 1991.

McISAAC, Joseph Patrick

Born August 20, 1888 in Antigonish, Nova Scotia, son of Angus McIsaac and Mary Power. His father was a Liberal Member of Parliament from Nova Scotia from 1853 until 1885 when he was appointed a judge. His Uncle, Colin Francis McIsaac, was also a Member of Parliament for Antigonish after serving in the Nova Scotia Cabinet.

McIsaac was educated in Antigonish where he attended Dalhousie University, graduating with a degree in Law.

McIsaac came to Alberta in 1912, where he settled in Camrose. During WWI, he enlisted in the Canadian Army and saw active service with the 52nd Battalion on the Western Front. Later, Captain McIsaac was a staff officer at the 3rd division headquarters.

Returning to Alberta in 1919, McIsaac was admitted to the Bar and then opened a law practice in Sexsmith in the Peace River Country. He was a prominent Northern Alberta lawyer for the next twenty-four years.

An active Liberal, Joseph P. McIsaac unsuccessfully contested Peace River in the 1926 Alberta general election, being defeated by Hugh Allen, the U.F.A. candidate.

Turning to federal politics, McIsaac unsuccessfully contested Peace River riding in the 1935 general election. The seat was won by Social Creditor Rene-Antoine Pelletier.

In September 1940, he was named Registrar of the Alberta Mobilization Board, a post he held for the next three years.

Justice Minister Louis St. Laurent appointed fifty-five year old Joseph P. McIsaac judge of the Northen Alberta District Court in November 1943.

Joseph Patrick McIsaac died August 20, 1963 at the age of seventy-five.

McIVOR, Donald Randolph

For many years, McIvor was a well-known Cowley Merchant.

Interested in federal politics, Donald Randolph McIvor, running as a Laurier-Liberal candidate, successfully contested the Macleod riding in the wartime 1917 general election. In a field of three candidates, he placed second, losing to the Unionist candidate Hugh M. Shaw.

Turning to provincial politics, McIvor, running as an Independent, unsuccessfully contested Pincher Creek in 1921.

In the early 1920s, he moved to Stettler where he became a prominent merchant. Still interested in obtaining a seat in the House of Commons, McIvor unsuccessfully contested the Camrose riding twice – First in 1926 and again in the 1930 federal election. On both occasions, W.T. Lucas, the U.F.A. incumbent, was elected.

In August 1939, the Camrose Federal Liberal Association passed a resolution requesting that the McKenzie King government appoint D.R. McIvor to the Senate. He was passed over and Dr. Aristide Blair of Edmonton was named to replace Pat Burns as a Senator from Alberta.

McKEEN, Charles Milton

Born May 10, 1885 in Fredericton, New Brunswick, son of W.G. McKeen and Mary Miles. Both his parents were of United Empire Loyalist stock.

C. Milton McKeen became a Rochfort farmer. During World War I, he enlisted in the Canadian Army and saw active service on the Western Front with the Canadian Seaforth Highlanders.

McKeen was returned as the U.F.A. member for the provincial Lac Ste. Anne constituency in 1921. He sat in the Legislature for 14 years as a private member on the government side of the chamber. He later served as a judge of the Calgary Juvenile Court for many years.

In 1911, he married Elizabeth A. Gunn, daughter of Peter Bunn, M.L.A. for Lac St. Anne from 1909 to 1921.

C. Milton McKeen died November 7, 1972. He was a Protestant.

McKINNEY, Louise Crummy

Born September 22, 1868 in Frankville, Ontario, one of the ten children of Richard Crummy, a Leeds County farmer and Esther Empey. Educated at Athens High School and Ottawa Normal School. McKinney taught in Ontario for four years before immigrating to the United States. In 1896, she married James William McKinney.

Coming to Western Canada from the United States in 1903, the McKinneys homesteaded near Claresholm. Louise McKinney became the President of the local branch of the Women's Christian Temperance Union [W.C.T.U.], and served as the Alberta President of the W.C.T.U. in 1908.

She was involved in the building of the first Methodist church in Claresholm. Mrs. McKinney was active in the formation of the United Church in the 1920s and was the only woman to sign the articles of union. She chaired the world meeting of the W.C.T.U. in 1931.

She became active in the movement to give women the vote in Alberta and was the first woman to be elected to the Legislature in 1917 with MacAdams. She was elected as a "Non-Partisan" candidate, mostly on a prohibition ticket and sat until 1921 when running as the U.F.A. candidate against Thomas Milnes, an Independent. In the legislature she supported legislation promoting welfare and public health. Mrs. McKinney was one of the "group of five" who appealed to the Privy Council in London and won the right for women to sit in the Senate.

Mrs. Louise McKinney died in Claresholm, Alberta on July 10, 1931 at the age of sixty-two.

(In 1917 it was said there was only one gentleman in the province - William Moffat – because he gave up his seat in the Legislature to a lady, Mrs. McKinney.)

McLAURIN, Colin Campbell

Born September 1, 1893 in Sarnia, Ontario, son of Rev. C.C. McLaurin, D.D., and Margaret Rosser. McLaurin was educated in Sarnia and Calgary. He had come to the province with his parents in 1907. On the outbreak of World War I, he joined the Army Engineers and later transferred to the Royal Air Force.

On his return to Canada, McLaurin came to Alberta to attend the University of Alberta, graduating with a degree in Law in 1922. He articled with the Calgary firm of Savary, Fenerty and Chadwick, before being admitted to the Bar in 1922.

For the next twenty years he was associated with the legal firm of Fenerty, McLaurin and Bessemer. He was awarded a K.C. in 1935.

An active Liberal, McLaurin unsuccessfully contested the federal riding of Calgary West in 1930. He was defeated by R.B. Bennett, the then National Conservative Leader who became the Prime Minister after the election.

Justice Minister Louis St. Laurent appointed him as a Justice of the Supreme Court, Trial Division in 1942. Ten years later he was named Chief Justice of the Supreme Court, Trial Division. He retired from the Bench in 1968. McLaurin was the first Chancellor of the University of Calgary (1966-1970).

Colin Campbell McLaurin died April 1981 in Calgary, at the age of eighty-eight.

McLENNAN, Andrew Robert

Born July 11, 1871 on a farm in Walkerton, Bruce County, Ontario, the eleventh of twelve children of Thomas McLennan and Barbara Little.

Educated in Walkerton, McLennan attended the London F.C.B.C. Business College. He was then employed in the manufacturing of lumber at Kenora, Ontario from 1897 to 1905. He next moved to Abernathy, Saskatchewan where he operated a lumberyard.

McLenna came to Alberta in 1912, where he settled in Edmonton and became a prominent businessman and influential citizen. He was a Proprietor of the Box and Shook Company and served as the President of the Edmonton branch of the Canadian Manufacturers Association.

Active in community affairs, McLennan served as an alderman from 1919 to 1921.

A Liberal, Andrew Robert McLennan successfully contested the five-member Edmonton constituency in 1921. In a field of twenty-six candidates, he placed first. In this election the Liberals won all five Edmonton seats. McLennan's four party running mates were John C. Bowlen (later the Lieutenant-Governor of Alberta); Mrs. Nellie McClung, the novelist; John R. Boyle (later the Justice of Alberta Supreme Court); and J.W. Hefferman, lawyer and Editor of "The Western Catholic." He sat in the Legislature as an active and vocal member of the opposition to the U.F.A. government for four years before resigning his seat.

Turning to federal politics, McLennan unsuccessfully contested the Edmonton East riding in the October 1925 general election. He was defeated by Conservative A.U.G. Bury. He also failed in the 1937 Edmonton East by-election.

Andrew Robert McLennan died April 9, 1943 in Edmonton at the age of seventy-three.

McLEOD, Donald

Born October 28, 1878, on the Isle of Lewis, Scotland, son of

Roderick McLeod and Ann MacDonald. Educated at Lewis, McLeod attended the Glasgow Technical College. In 1903, he married Margaret, daughter of Torguil MacLeod of Kenock, Isle of Lewis. They had five daughters and a son.

Coming to Alberta in 1910, McLeod became a prominent Lake Isle district farmer. He was named a Director and Secretary of Alberta Live Stock Producers. He was an active member of the United Farmers of Alberta Movement.

Donald McLeod became a U.F.A. member for the provincial Stony Plain constituency in 1930. He sat in the Legislature for five years. In 1935, he was defeated by Social Creditor William E. Hayes.

McLeod was a Presbyterian.

McPHERSON, Oran Leo "Tony"

Born April 12, 1886 in Kingsman, Kansas, son of Taylor McPherson and Eliza Davidson, both of whom were Americans of Scotch descent. Educated at Alton's Skurtle College, McPherson attended the University of Illinois for two years.

McPherson, with his two brothers, came to Alberta in 1907 where they settled near Vulcan. During his time in Vulcan, McPherson became a prominent farmer. He was one of the founders of the United Farmers of Alberta organization in 1909 and a close friend of the long-time U.F.A. President Henry Wise Wood. He operated a 3,000-acre wheat farm. In 1919, he was named President of the U.F.A. provincial political association.

Oran Leo "Tony" McPherson was returned the U.F.A. member for the provincial Little Bow constituency in 1921. He sat in the Legislature for the next fourteen years. In 1922, he was named Speaker of the Alberta Legislative Assembly. He held this position for four years. Premier Brownlee appointed McPherson Minister of the Public Works on December 31, 1926. He held this portfolio until Premier Brownlee resigned in July 1934. Premier Reid did not appoint McPherson in his Cabinet, and so he became a private member.

In the 1935 Alberta election, McPherson failed his re-election bid. He placed second, losing to Social Creditor, Rev. Peter Dawson by a 1,618-vote margin. He then retired from politics at the age of forty-nine and returned to farming. However, he took an active part in local organization.

McPherson was married twice. His first marriage, in 1908, was to Cora Farmer, formerly of Ashley, Illinois and ended in a much-publicized divorce in 1931. Together, McPherson and Farmer had four sons. Secondly, in 1932, McPherson married Mrs. Helen Mattern (nee Gordon). At the time, it was said that the divorce ruined his political career.

Oran Leo "Tony" MvPherson died May 23, 1949 in Victoria at the age of sixty-three. The Canadian Who's Who (1936-1937) says he was "quiet, unassuming, yet forceful; guided by well determined convictions."

MIHALCHEON, George M.

Born October 1, 1893 at Borau, Bukovina, son of Michael Mihalcheon and Kate Harasim, both ethnic Romanians.

He came to the District of Alberta, N.W.T. as a child in 1901 and was educated at Vegreville. He then qualified as a teacher at the Camrose Normal School. He then taught rural schools. Later he also farmer and became a Borau Merchant.

George M. Mihalcheon was returned as the U.F.A. member for the provincial Whitford constituency in 1926. He sat in the Legislature for four years as a private member on the government side of the chamber. In 1930 he did not seek re-election but retired from politics.

In 1921 he married Mary Lutzak. They had three daughters.

George Mihalcheon died in October 1956.

MISKEW, Peter

Born November 27, 1899 in Biliawce, Galicia, son of Wasyl Miskey and Tekla Wojtowycz. He was of Ukrainian ethnic descent. His father served in the Austrian Army.

Miskew came to the District of Alberta, N.W.T. as a child with his parents in 1902, the family homesteaded in St. Michel. Educated in Mundare, and on the advice of his parish priest, Fr. Kryzanowski, young Miskew studied for a time in the St. Albert Seminary. He then qualified as a teacher in Edmonton. He became a teacher and later he attended the University of Alberta, graduating with a degree in Arts and then preceded to obtain a Master's degree. He was a high school teacher at Smoky Lake for a number of years.

Peter A. Miskew became a U.F.A. member for the provincial Victoria constituency in 1930. He sat in the Legislature for five years. In 1935, he did not seek re-election but retired from politics at the age of thirty-six.

In 1936 he was admitted to the Alberta Bar. Miskew became a lawyer and practiced law in Edmonton.

Peter Miskew died September, 1965 in Edmonton.

MONTAINBAULT, Hyacinthe

Montainbault was of French-Canadian descent. Born in Québec, he became a homestead inspector.

Hyacinthe Montainbeault ran twice, unsuccessfully: first as the U.F.A. candidate for the Beave River constituency in 1921 and then as a Liberal for the provincial St. Paul constituency in 1926.

Hyacinthe Montainbeault died May 30, 1930, while still a young man. He was a Roman Catholic.

MOORE, Alex

Born October 1, 1874 in Lion's Head, Ontario, son of Robert Moore and Isabella Kidd, Moore was educated at the Lion's Head School.

In 1903, Moore married Anna M. Wetherland of Cape Chin, Ontario. His wife's father, Alexander Wetherland, had moved to Alberta several years prior. The Moores moved to join him in 1906. They homesteaded in the Dog Pound district northwest of Calgary. Ten years later he purchased a dairy farm near Cochrane.

In 1919, Moore was nominated as the the U.F.A. candidate to contest the Cochrane by-election. The vacancy was caused by the death of C.W. Fisher, the Speaker of the Legislature. He won Pound's postmaster Edward V. Thompson, to become the first U.F.A. member of the Legislature. He was re-elected in the formation of the U.F.A.

government under the Premiership of Herbert Greenfield. He was unhappy at not having been taken into the Cabinet.

His political career ended in 1926, when his Model T. Ford automobile became stuck in a mud hole and prevented him from filing his nomination papers on time. He operated his dairy farm until 1943 when he retired.

Alex Moore died in 1952 at the age of seventy-eight. He was a Presbyterian.

MORISSEY, Joseph P.

Born on a St. Albert farm, Morissey attended the University of Alberta, graduating in 1928.

Joseph P. Morissey ran unsuccessfully as the U.F.A. candidate for the provincial St. Albert constituency in 1935.

In 1970, he was employed by the Director of the Alberta Catholic Schools Association in Edmonton.

MUIR, Donald Stuart

He became a prominent Leduc farmer.

Donald Stuart Muir ran unsuccessfully as the U.F.A. candidate for the provincial Leduc constituency in 1921. He lost to Liberal incumbent Stan G. Tobin by a narrow ten-vote margin.

NORMANDEAU, Louis

Born in 1897 in Beauharnois, Quebec. Educated at the Beauharnois College.

Came to Alberta as a young man in 1910, he homesteaded in the Lac La Biche district, when the settlement was 125 miles from the nearest railway line. Later he farmed at Legal and then at Westlock before finally settling near Morinville. He became a prominent farmer.

Active in the U.F.A. Movement, Normandeau was nominated to be the party's candidate for St. Albert in 1926, edging out the U.F.A. member of the previous Legislature, Telesphore St. Arneaud as well as Omen St. Germain and M. Sequin.

Louis Normandeau ran twice, unsuccessfully: first as the U.F.A. candidate for the provincial St. Albert constituency in 1921 and again as the U.F.A. candidate for the federal Athabasca riding in the March 21, 1932 by-election. In a field of four candidates, he placed third. Conservative Percy G. Davies won the seat.

Normandeau was well known in agricultural circles for forty years. He was a Roman Catholic.
(In 1962, he was still farming near Morinville.)

PARLBY, Mrs. Mary Irene

Born January 9, 1868 in London, England, daughter of Lt. Colonel Ernest L. Marryat and Elizabeth Lynch, Mary Irene Marryat was educated privately in London. Her grandfather was a member of the British Parliament while her uncle, Captain Frederick Marryat, was an author. In 1897, Parlby married Walter Coventry Hall Parlby, in London. Her husband was a graduate of the Oxford University.

Parlby and her husband came to Alberta as pioneer homesteaders in the Alix district. Mrs. Parlby became active in the United Farmers of Alberta (U.F.A.) Movement, serving as the provincial President of the United Women of Alberta from 1915 to 1919. She sat on the provincial Executive. This group became the nucleus of the Cabinet.

Mrs. M. Irene Parlby returned as the member for the provincial

Ponoka constituency. She sat in the Legislature for the next fourteen years. Premier Greenfield took her into his Cabinet as Minister without Portfolio, a position she retained until 1935. Parlby was not a candidate in 1935. She shares credit for the successful campaign of five Alberta women in the petition to the British Judicial Committee of the Privy Council for the judgment that resulted in Women's eligibility for membership in the Canadian Senate.

Mary Irene Parlby was awarded an honorary Doctorate from the University of Alberta in 1935 - the first woman so honored.

Mary Irene Parlby died July 12, 1965 in Red Deer, Alberta

(See: The Canadian Who's Who, 1936-1937)

PETERSON, Lawrence

Born April 12, 1878 in Provo, Utah, son of Andrew Peterson, a pioneer Danish Mormon settler of the intermountain region. Lawrence Peterson was educated at Provo and Brigham Young University.

Peterson homesteaded in the Barnwell district of the District of Alberta, N.W.T. in 1902 and became a well-known farmer and Chairman of the Taber Irrigation District. He was a Director of the United Farmers of Alberta from 1919 to 1922.

Lawrence Peterson was returned as the member for the provincial Taber constituency in 1921. He sat in the Legislature for nine years. In 1930, Peterson failed to win the U.F.A. nomination. He did run as an Independent but was defeated by the U.F.A. candidate J.J. McLellan.

Lawrence Peterson then retired from politics to his farm. Peterson died September 7, 1951 in Taber.

PITMAN, Col. Ernest A.

Born in 1886, Pitman was educated in England.

Pitman came to Alberta in 1908 as a young man. He first settled in Edmonton where he worked. Later he homesteaded in the Chauvin district where he became a well-known farmer. During WWI, he enlisted in the Canadian Army and saw active service on the Western Front.

After the war, he returned to Chauvin where he lived for the next forty years.

Active in the militia in the 1930s, Pitman was the officer commanding the 19th Alberta Dragoons for a number of years.

Interested in provincial politics, Major Ernest A. Pitman, running as an Independent, unsuccessfully contested Wainwright in 1930. He was defeated by J. Russell Love, the U.F.A. incumbent by a 310-vote margin on the final count.

Turning to federal politics, Col. Ernest A. Pitman, running this time as a Liberal, unsuccessfully contested the Battle River riding in the 1940 wartime election. He was defeated by incumbent Social Creditor Robert Fair.

During WWII, Pitman re-enlisted in the Canadian Army and served on the "Home Front" due to his age.

Ernest A. Pitman died in 1959 in Chauvin at the age of seventy-three.

PLUMER, Benjamin Smith

Born May 7, 1889 in Chadwick, Illinois, U.S.A. Plumer's father had moved from New Hampshire to a quarter section in Illinois. His ancestors had come from England. He was raised on a farm.

Plumer came to Alberta in 1911 and settled at Bassano, where he became an agricultural implement and machinery dealer. He became a provincial Executive member of the United Farmers of Alberta.

Ben S. Plumer ran unsuccessfully as the U.F.A. candidate for the provincial Bow Valley constituency in 1926. He placed second, losing on the final count by one vote to Alberta Liberal leader Captain Joseph T. Shaw.

From 1943 to 1957, Plumer served as Chairman of the Alberta Wheat Pool Board of Directors, as a member of the Grain Committee of the Board of Grain Commissioners and also a member of The Advisory Committee to the Canadian Wheat Board. In 1912, Pitman married Florence M. Cleary, formerly of Chadwick in Moose Jaw.

PROUDFOOT, Lorne

Born October 8, 1880 in Fenaghvale, Ontario, son of James Proudfoot and Sarah F. Bradley. His father was of Scotch descent and his mother was of Irish descent. Educated at Regina Normal School and Vankleek Hill Collegiate Institute, he qualified as a teacher.

Coming to Alberta, he became a prominent Chinook farmer. He served as Secretary- Treasurer of the Collholme Municipal District and Secretary-Treasurer of the Chinook School District.

He ran unsuccessfully as an Independent candidate in the 1917 Alberta general election. After this, he became active in the United Farmers of Alberta Movement.

Lorne Proudfoot was returned as the member for the provincial Acadia constituency in 1921. He sat in the Legislature for 14 years. In 1935 he was defeated by Social Creditor Norman B. James.

Lorne Proudfoot then retired from politics to spend his remaining time on his farm. He died in 1977.

PYE, Ronald

Ronald Pye became a well-known Penhold farmer.

Pye unsuccessfully ran as the U.F.A. candidate for the provincial Innisfail constituency in 1935.

REID, Richard Gavin

Born January 17, 1879 in Glasgow, Scotland, son of George Reid and Margaret Ogston. Reis was educated at Glasgow's Hutcheson's Grammar School. He apprenticed to a dry goods merchant, subsequently taking charge of the retail store. During the South African War, he enlisted in the British Army, and saw active service with the Medical Corps on the veldt.

Immigrating to Canada in 1902, the young Richard Reid first farmed in southern Manitoba before becoming a lumberjack. He became a prominent farmer and took an active part in the formation of the United Farmers of Alberta. Active in community affairs, he served first as a councilor and then as the reeve of Buffalo Coulee municipal district. He also served on the local Hospital Board. In 1919, he married Marion Stuart of Manville. They had three sons and a daughter.

Richard Gavin Reid was returned as the member of the provincial Vermillion constituency in 1921. He sat in the Legislature for fourteen years first as a Cabinet Minister and then as the Premier. Premier Greenfield appointed him Minister of Municipal Affairs and Minister of Health. In 1923, he was transferred from the Health field to become the Provincial Treasurer. In 1926, when John Brownlee became Premier, Reid was reappointed Provincial Treasurer and Minister of Municipal Affairs.

On July 10, 1934, on the resignation of Brownlee, Richard Gavin Reid became Alberta's sixth Premier. The Financial Post at the time said: "Premier Reid was too thorough in his thinking to be extremist; too deliberate to be a radical; too human to be a reactionary".

Despite introducing debt adjustment legislation, Premier Reid and all his U.F.A. members of the Legislature were defeated in the Social Credit sweep in the August 1935 election. Reid then retired from politics at the age of fifty-six, returning to his Buffalo Coulee farm. Later he became a company executive.

Richard Gavin Reid died October 18, 1980, at the advanced age of one hundred and one. He was a Presbyterian.

(See: The Canadian Who's Who, 1953)

ROBINSON, C.W.

C.W. Robinson became a prominent Hand Hills farmer. He was Commanding Officer – Lieutenant Colonel – of the 187th (Central Alberta) Battalion.

C.W. Robinson unsuccessfully ran as the U.F.A. candidate for the Hand Hills constituency in 1935.

RONNING, Chester Alvin

Born December 13, 1894 in Frencheng, Hueph, China, son of Halvor Ronning, a Lutheran Missionary and Hannah Rorem.

As a child, Ronning came to Alberta with his parents, who returned to their old home in Camrose. Educated in Camrose, Ronning attended the Camrose Normal School, qualifying as a teacher. During World War I, he enlisted in the Royal Air Force and saw action as a pilot on the Western Front.

After the war, Chester Ronning taught school in Edmonton for three years before going to China as a Lutheran Missionary.

In 1927, he returned to take up the position of Principal of the Camrose Lutheran College. He held this post for the next fifteen years.

Chester A. Ronning was returned the U.F.A. member for the provincial Camrose constituency in the October 25, 1932 by-election. He sat in the Legislature for three years as a "left wing" U.F.A. backbencher. In 1935, Ronning was defeated by Social Creditor, William N. Chant. He was also unsuccessful at the polls in the 1940 general election and the 1942 by-election, caused by the death of Social Credit Cabinet Minister, Duncan Mullen – on both occasions, he ran as the C.C.F. candidate.

For a brief period, Ronning was the Alberta leader of the C.C.F. In 1942, he enlisted in the Canadian Air Force, and served as an intelligence officer for the duration. After the war, he joined the Canadian Diplomatic Corps. During the next twenty years, he held numerous foreign postings including being stationed at the Canadian Embassy at Nanking, China, Minister to Normay, Ambassador to Norway and High Commissioner to India.

In 1965, Ronning retired from the diplomatic service. For years, Chester Ronning was recognized as an expert to Chinese affairs. He received an honorary degree from the University of Lethbridge in 1971.

Chester A. Ronning died December 31, 1984 in Camrose.

ROSS, Alex A.

Born January 15, 1880 in Premnoy, Scotland, son of James Ross and Jessie Thompson. Educated in Oyne, Aberdeenshire, he became a stonemason by trade.

In 1906, Ross came to Canada as a young man and he finally settled in Calgary and worked as a stonemason. He became active in the Labor Movement in the city.

Alex A. Ross was returned as the Labor member for Calgary Centre in 1917. He sat in the Legislature for nine years. In 1921, he headed the polls in the five-member Calgary constituency. Premier Greenfield asked him to join the U.F.A. Cabinet as Minister of Public Works and Labor. He was returned by acclamation in the December 1921 Calgary by-election. He was the only non-U.F.A. member of the Cabinet.

In the June 1926 general election, Alex Ross was defeated. He resigned from the Cabinet on December 30, 1926. He was then appointed Chairman of the Workman's Compensation Board and held the position for a number of years. He moved to Victoria in 1938.

Alex A. Ross died July 17, 1953 in Victoria at the age of seventy-three. He was never married.

RUSSELL, Charles Homer

Born in 1877 in Exeter, Ontario, son of William Russell and Jean Moir. His Scottish-born father was a farmer.

Educated in Exeter and Goderich, Russell attended the University of Toronto, graduating with a degree in Arts and preceded to qualify as a teacher.

Russell came to the District of Alberta, N.W.T. in 1903, where he taught school for some years. Russell was then a school inspector prior to taking up the study of Law in an Edmonton Law office. He was admitted to the Bar in 1914.

Russell settled in Wetaskiwin, where he formed a legal partnership with W.H. O'Dell. He was a prominent Wetaskiwin lawyer for the next twenty years. He was the City Solicitor for a number of years.

A Conservative, Charles Homer Russell unsuccessfully contested the federal riding of Wetaskiwin on four occasions – 1925, 1926, 1930 and 1940. He came closer to winning the seat in 1930, when he was defeated by incumbent U.F.A., William Irvine, by 424 votes.

RYAN, Edward F.

Ryan was born in 1876 in Charlottetown, P.E.I, where he was educated and qualified as a lawyer.

Ryan came to Alberta in 1906 where he settled in Calgary and joined the legal firm of "Paddy" Nolan.

Ryan was one of the most prominent lawyers in Alberta and was awarded a K.C. in 1921.

In 1920, the Liberal of Calgary West federal riding nominated City Commissioner, A.J. Samis. In a second nomination meeting, Edward F. Ryan was named the Liberal candidate, but he later withdrew his nomination.

Ryan unsuccessfully contested the federal riding of Calgary West in 1925. In a field of three candidates, he placed third. The seat was won by Labor candidate, Captain Joseph T. Shaw who edged out the incumbent R.B. Bennett by 16 votes.

Edward F. Ryan died November 17, 1929 in Rochester, Minnesota at the age of fifty-three.

ST. ARNAUD, Telespore

Born December 15, 1870 in Ste. Genevieve, Québec, son of Joseph St. Arnaud and Rose Trottier. He was of French descent. Educated in St. Boniface, Manitoba. He became a well- known Vimy farmer.

Telespore St. Arnaud was returned as the U.F.A. member for the provincial St. Albert constituency in 1921. He sat in the Legislature for five years as a private member on the government side of the chamber. In 1903 he married the daughter of Paul Normandeau of Beauharnois. They had five daughters and three sons. He was a Roman Catholic.

ST. GERMAIN, Omer

Born September 14, 1977 in St. Pie de Ouire, Québec, son of Benonie St. Germain and Christine Plante, both French-Canadians. Educated at the Nicolet Seminary, obtaining a Bachelor of Arts.

Omer St. Germain came to the District of Alberta, N.W.T. with his parents as a child in 1890. The St. Germain family homesteaded near Leduc. Educated in Leduc, he attended the Nicolet Seminary and Trois Rivière College. He then attended Laval University, graduating in Law in 1905. Returning to Alberta, St. Germain articled in Edmonton and was admitted to the Bar in 1905. Omer St. Germain then established a legal practice in Morinville in 1907, where he became a prominent French Canadian lawyer.

Active in community affairs he served as the Mayor of Morinville on three occasions. From 1909 to 1912 he was the Publisher of "Le Progrès," a French-language newspaper. For many years, he was Secretary-Treasurer of the community.

In 1908, St. Germain married Alice Reneault of St. Albert. Together they conceived one son, Gerard St. Germain.

Interested in politics, St. Germain contested unsuccessfully as a Conservative in the constituency of St. Albert in 1909, being defeated by Liberal, Lucien Boudreau. In a field of three candidates, he placed last and forfeited his deposit. He contested the same constituency successfully in 1930 as a U.F.A. candidate, defeating Liberal incumbent Boudreau. In 1933, after the election of Chester Ronning as U.F.A. member for Camrose, St. Germain crossed the floor of the Chamber to sit as a Liberal. Peter Miskew, U.F.A. member for Victoria, accompanied him. St. Germain gave two reasons for his change in political sides. First of all, he was unimpressed with the failure of Premier Brownlee to demand the resignation of Public Works Minister, O.L. McPherson. Secondly, St. Germain was upset over the failure of the government to make clear its position in connection with the U.F.A. platform, adopted at the 1933 annual convention, regarding the socialization of all industries including land. He sat until defeated in 1935 by Social Creditor, Charles Holder. He then returned to his Morinville law practice. In 1948, St. Germain ran unsuccessfully in the provincial St. Albert constituency.

Omer St. Germain died February 11, 1945 at the age of sixty-seven. He was Roman Catholic.

SANDERS, Albert Leroy

Born May 22, 1889 in Tory, Idaho, son of Thomas G. Sanders

and Alice Mary Stinson. Both his parents were Canadian by birth and the family was of Scotch descent. Sanders was educated in Troy.

Sanders came to Alberta as a young man in 1909 and homesteaded in the Foreman district near Stettler. He became a well-known farmer and was a strong supporter of the United Farmers of Alberta Movement.

In 1916, Sanders married Eva Pearl Dobson, formerly of Orofino, Idaho. Albert Leroy Sanders was returned as the member for the provincial Stettler constituency in 1921. He sat in the Legislature for fourteen years. In 1935, he was defeated by Social Creditor, Charles Cockroft.

He was a Presbyterian.

SCHOOLING, Lacky P.

Born in 1880 in Missouri, U.S.A., of German parents. Schooling was trained as a Lutheran Minister. He served as the Lutheran Minister in Pullman, Washington, for several years.

Schooling came to Alberta in 1910 and homesteaded in Standard. He became a Hussar businessman and farmer. Active in the U.F.A. Movement, he assisted in the organization of the Wheat Pool.

Lacky P. Schooling ran unsuccessfully as the U.F.A. candidate for the provincial Bow Valley constituency in 1930. He placed second, losing to independent J. MacKintosh.

Shortly after, he was permanently injured in a farm accident, being crushed by a tractor. He was still farming in 1960.

SCRATCH, Alec Carman

Born in 1877 in Blysewood, Ontario of United Empire Loyalist stock. His ancestors had come from Pennsylvania in 1782. Scratch was educated in Leamington, near his hometown.

Scratch came to the District of Alberta, N.W.T. in 1901, where he helped build schools on an Indian reserve before he went to Calgary where he took Accounting at Garbutt Business College.

Later, Scratch was the proprietor of a livery stable in Irricana. By 1917, he was a CPR real estate agent and part owner of a dairy farm near Irricana.

Active in community affairs, Scratch served as reeve of the Keoman municipal district in the 1920s and was also active in the United Farmers of Alberta Movement.

Interested in federal politics, Alec Carman Scratch, running as an Independent Conservative, unsuccessfully contested the Bow River riding in the 1926 general election. He was defeated by E.J. Garland by a 2,116-vote margin.

In 1956, Scratch moved to Penticton, B.C.

Alec Carman Scratch died November 20, 1968 in Penticton at the advanced age of ninety-one.

SHARPE, Major Wallace J.

Born on August 31, 1889 at the Pincher Creek rectory, son of early southern Alberta pioneers, Emma and Sam Sharpe. Educated in Pincher Creek, he became a well-known Lundbreck rancher.

At the outbreak of World War I, Sharpe enlisted in the Canadian Army and was one of the original officers of the 3rd Canadian Mounted Rifles. In 1915, he volunteered for a draft that proceeded to the Western Front with the Fort Garry Horse. Major Sharpe had a distinguished military career. He was the adjutant of his regime and was awarded the Military Cross and the Distinguished Service Order. Sharpe was wounded at Cambrai in November 1917. His efforts would result in the amputation of his left leg. He was demobilized in 1918. He was a war hero.

Major Wallace J. Sharpe ran unsuccessfully as the U.F.A. candidate for the provincial Rocky Mountain constituency in 1921.

He died January 12, 1923 at Lundbreck Ranch at the age of thirty-four. He was married and had one son, Ernest Sharpe.

SHAW, Joseph Tweed

Born August 30, 1883 in Port Arthur, Ontario, son of Joseph Shaw and Eliza Coulter.

Came to the District of Alberta, N.W.T. as a child, where his family settled in Calgary.

Educated in Calgary, Shaw attended the Regina Normal School, qualifying as a teacher. He then taught in Penhold.

Later he attended the University of Michigan, graduating with a degree in Law. In 1912, Shaw was admitted to the Alberta Bar and joined the Calgary Legal firm of Short, Ross, Shaw and Maywood. He became a prominent Alberta lawyer, and was awarded a K.C.

During WWI, he enlisted in the Canadian Army and saw active service as a Captain with the 46th Battalion on the Western Front. He was seriously wounded at Vimy Ridge in April 1917 and was awarded the Military Cross for his part in the battle. He was demobilized in 1919 and returned to his Calgary law practice.

Interested in federal politics, Joseph T. Shaw, running as a Labor candidate, successfully contested the Calgary West riding in the 1921 general election. In an upset election, he defeated R.B. Bennett, the acting Minister of Justice by a narrow 16-vote margin. He sat in Parliament for four years as a private member on the opposition benches. While in the Commons, Shaw sponsored an amendment to the Divorce Act that permitted a wife to obtain a divorce for the same causes as those on which a husband could obtain a divorce.

In the 1925 federal election, Shaw, running with Liberal endorsement, was defeated by R.B. Bennett who had a 4,216-vote majority.

Turning to provincial politics, Captain Shaw was named the Alberta Liberal Leader, replacing C.R. Mitchell, who had been appointed to the Bench.

In the 1926 Alberta election, he successfully contested Bow Valley. He won the seat with a one-vote margin, defeating Ben Plumer, the U.F.A. candidate.

Joseph Tweed Shaw died July 12, 1944.

SHIELD, William Hetherington

Born July 12, 1878 in Carr Shield, Northumberland, England, son of Thomas Shield and Mary Hetherington.

Shield came to Canada as a youth in 1898 and he settled in Alberta seven years later where he became a prominent Macleod farmer. He became active in the United Farmers of Alberta Movement.

William H. Shield was returned as the member for the provincial Macleod constituency in 1921. He sat in the Legislature for 14 years. In 1935 he was defeated by Social Creditor James Hartly.

He then retired from politics to his farm. He belonged to the United Church. He was a Methodist.

SMITH, George Wilbert

Born April 24, 1855 in Maitland, Nova Scotia, son of Morris Smith and Ann Gaetz. His father was English while his mother was German. Educated in Maitland, Smith qualified as a teacher. He taught in the Maritimes for a number of years.

Smith came to the District of Alberta, N.W.T. in 1883 and was an early pioneer of the Red Deer district. He was the first schoolteacher in central Alberta. He taught a number of years before going into business. Smith played an active role in the development of Red Deer. Active in civic affairs, he served for a number of years on the town council before being elected the Mayor in 1917. He was also Chairman of the school board. He became a prominent businessman. He was the President of Smith Land Company and a Director of Western General Electric.

Smith was married to the eldest daughter of Rev. Leo Gaetz, pioneer Methodist missionary and founder of Red Deer. They had four sons and four daughters. One daughter married James G. La France and another Edgar G. Johns.

George Wilbert Smith was returned as the U.F.A. member for the provincial Red Deer constituency in 1921. Smith sat in the Legislature until the time of his death.

George Wilber Smith died August 1, 1931 in Red Deer at the age of seventy-six.

SMITH, Nelson Stuart

Born April 19, 1888 in Minto, Manitoba, son of Charles Solomon Smith and Emma Sparrow. He was of English descent. Educated in Minto, he attended the Manitoba Agricultural College at Winnipeg, graduating in Science.

Smith came to Alberta, and was an instructor at the Olds Agricultural College and a well- known farmer. He served as President of the Alberta Milk and Cream Producers Association.

Nelson S. Smith was returned as the U.F.A. member for the provincial Olds constituency in 1921, defeating Liberal Agriculture Minister Duncan Marshall. In the 1926 Alberta general election, he defeated Liberal candidate Norman Cook and Conservative L.H Walkley. He sat in the Legislature for four years as a private member on the government side of the chamber. In 1930, he did not seek re-election but retired from politics.

In 1913, he married Zeta Irene Brown of Spirling Manitoba. They had one daughter. He was a Methodist.

SMITH, Vernon Winfield

Born February 17, 1864 in Pownal, Prince Edward Island, son of John Smith and Amelia Gay. Educated at Pownal, he attended the Charlottetown Business College.

Smith came to the Northwest Territories as a young man. Smith was on railway construction crews all across the prairies and the United States northwest for a number of years. In time he became a valuable employee of a famous railway-contracting firm of Foley, Welsh and Stewart of Vancouver. He played a vital role in the completing of the Grand Trunk Pacific tracks through the Rocky Mountains.

Leaving railway construction, smith came to Alberta and acquired land in the Camrose district, where he became a well-known farmer and breeder of Herefords.

Vernon Winfield Smith was returned the U.F.A. member for the provincial Camrose constituency in 1921 and he defeated the Liberal Cabinet Minister, George P. Smith (no relation). Premier Greenfield immediately took him into the Cabinet as the Minster of Railway and Telephones; he was also in charge of irrigation. He sat in the Legislature and retained these two portfolios until the time of his death.

Vernon Winfield Smith died July 19, 1932 in Edmonton at the age of sixty-eight. At the time of his death, Premier Brownlee stated that: "Smith was one of our most valuable Ministers. He was largely instrumental in the tremendous advantage reaped by the province in the sale of the Northen Alberta Railway, which brought the province some 26 million dollars". His son is Justice V.W. MacBraire Smith of the Alberta Court of Queen's Bench and later a Justice of Alberta Court of Approval.

SMITH, William Cunningham

Born July 12, 1875 in Glanallen, Ontario, son of Abram Smith and Eliza Cunningham. He was of Irish descent. Educated at the Stratford Collegiate Institute, he qualified as a dentist in Winnipeg and Denver. He practiced his profession for several years in Denver.

During the South African War, Smith enlisted with the Canadian Mounted Rifles and saw active service on the veldt. As a Boer War veteran he received a grant of land.

Coming to Alberta, Smith became a Medicine Hat farmer and rancher. In 1907,he married Evelyn Rutherford of Perth County Ontario. They had a son and a daughter. He became active in the United Farmers of Alberta Movement.

William C. Smith was returned as the member for the provincial Empress constituency in 1921. He sat in the Legislature for 14 years. In 1935 he was defeated by Social Creditor David Lush.

After his defeat, he retired from politics to his farm. He was a Presbyterian.

SPARKS, Evert Ellsworth

Born September 10, 1879 in Mound Valley, Kansas, U.S.A., son of Joel W. Sparks and Addied Stevenson. He was an America of Scotch ancestry.

Sparks came to Alberta in 1910 and became a Wetaskiwin farmer. Active in the formation of the U.F.A., he served as a Director in 1915 and 1916.

Evert Ellsworth Sparks was returned as the U.F.A. member for the provincial Wetaskiwin constituency in 1921. He sat in the Legislature for five years. In 1926, he was defeated by Liberal Hugh

John Montgomery who had held the seat from 1914 to 1921.

SPEAKMAN, Alfred

Born August 24, 1880 in Dundee, Scotland, son of James Speakman and Mary Hanna Farrar, both of whom were English by birth.

As a child, Speakman came to the District of Alberta, N.W.T. in 1891 with his parents. His father homesteaded in the Red Deer district. Educated at Red Deer, Speakman left school at sixteen to homestead on a quarter section near his father's farm.

James Speakman and his son were prominent in the formation of the United Farmers of Alberta Movement in 1919. Speakman was the President of the farmers' organization in 1913. Alfred Speakman became a prominent farmer and active in the furthering of farmer's interests.

Alfred Speakman was returned as the Progressive (U.F.A.) member for the federal Red Deer riding in 1921. He defeated William W.B. McInnes, a former British Columbia judge by an 8,205-vote margin. Speakman sat in Parliament as a private member on the opposition benches for fourteen years. During that time, he was the Chairman of the House of Commons Committee on Soldier Settlement. He was re-elected in 1925, 1926 and 1930. In the 1935 federal election, Speakman was defeated by Social Creditor Eric Poole.

Turning to provincial politics, Alfred Speakman, running as an Independent, successfully contested Red Deer constituency in 1940. He sat in the Legislature for three years as one of the rotating House Leaders of the Independent anti-Social Credit group.

Alfred Speakman died November 4, 1943 in Edmonton while still a sitting member of the Legislature at the age of sixty-three. He was a Methodist who joined the United Church. (His nephew, James Stanley Speakman (1906-1962) was the Progressive Conservative Member of Parliament for Red Deer from 1950 until his death four years later.)

SPENCER, Henry Elvins

Born March 2, 1882 in Albester, Warwickshire, England, son of William Spencer and Mary Elvins. His ancestors had been yeomen farmers for generations. He was a Unitarian. Educated in Albester, he attended the Wolverley Collegiate before he was employed by a bank at Stratford-on-Avon in 1899. He was a bank clerk for six years. In 1906, he went to France where he worked in the printing and publishing trade for two years.

Spencer came to Alberta in 1908 with his brother, Herbert Spencer, and they homesteaded near Edgerton. When they arrived, the nearest railway line was fifty miles away; it took a team of oxen two and a half days from the railroad to their sod shack.

The Spencer brothers became prominent farmers and they became active in the United Farmers of Alberta Movement. Henry E. Spencer was a U.F.A. Director from 1917 to 1921. Active in community affairs, Henry E. Spencer was the first Secretary-Treasurer of the School District. He held this position for several years.

Henry Elvin Spencer was returned the member for the federal Battle River riding in 1921. He defeated Liberal lawyer Henry Vernon Fieldhouse by a 10,521-vote margin. He sat in Parliament for fourteen years as an active member of the “Ginger” Progressive opposition group. Spencer was the Progressive party whip for most of the period. In 1935, he was defeated by Social Creditor Robert Fair. He retired from politics to his farm.

In the 1940s Spencer was elected to the Wainwright School Division and served as Chairman. In 1947, he was named President of the Alberta School Trustees Association. He was also the deputy reeve of the Municipal district for a number of years. In 1948, he retired from farming in the Edgerton district and joined his brother in Comox, B.C. In later years, he was active in the World Federalist Movement. In 1913, he married Harriet Zelia Crowe. They gave birth to Elvin Yuill Spencer, who later became a researcher chemist and achieved his doctorate.

Henry Elvins Spencer died October 1, 1972 at the age of ninety-one.

(See: Canadian Who’s Who, 1935-1936)

STEVENS, Wilbert A.

Wilbert Stevens was born in 1898 at St. Mary's, Ontario.

In 1906, Stevens came to Alberta with his parents; his father homesteaded in the Wetaskiwin district.

Educated in Wetaskiwin, Stevens attended Brandon College, Manitoba, graduating with a a degree in Arts in 1930. It was while at Brandon, that Stevens became a Socialist. (Two of his classmates were Stanley Knowles, long-time Member of Parliament for Winnipeg North Centre and Thomas Douglas, the former N.D.P. National leader).

Stevens later became a Wetaskiwin farmer.

In 1935, Stevens was nominated the U.F.A. candidate for Wetaskiwin. He declared "that there was a possibility of building a new social order based upon human values. The profit motif must go, and society must establish or work out a complete re-orientation of ideals."

He unsuccessfully ran for the provincial Wetaskiwin constituency in 1935, and twice he unsuccessfully ran as the C.C.F. candidate for the federal Wetaskiwin riding in 1945 and again in 1949.

STEWART, Dr. John Smith

Born May 18, 1878 in Brampton, Ontario, son of John Stewart and Mary Armstrong. Educated in Brampton, Stewart attended the University of Toronto, graduating with a D.D.S. in 1903. He established a dental practice in Lethbridge. He was a prominent city resident for the next sixty-seven years.

Prior to that, Stewart had seen active service in the Boer War as a private in Lord Strathcona's Horse. During the Great War, he commanded the Artillery Brigade Canadian Expeditionary Force in France. He was then promoted to General of the Third Canadian Division. He was awarded the DSO and the Croix de Guerre. He was twice wounded and twice mentioned in dispatches and he was a Brigadier General from 1917 to 1919.

A Conservative, Stewart contested successfully the 1911

Lethbridge by-election, caused when W.A. Buchanan resigned the seat to enter federal politics. He sat in the Legislature until he resigned in 1925. Interested in federal politics, Dr. John S. Stewart unsuccessfully contested the Lethbridge riding in the 1925 general elections. He was defeated by U.F.A. incumbent Lincoln H. Jelliff by a 743-vote margin. He sat in Parliament for five years as a private member on the opposition benches. In 1935, he failed in his re-election bid when Social Creditor John Blackmore was elected.

John Smith Stewart died August 14, 1970 in Lethbridge at the age of ninety-two.

STRASHOK, Fred

Born in 1908 on a farm near St. Michael, fifty miles northeast of Edmonton. His parents had come to the District of Alberta, N.W.T. in 1897 from Eastern Europe to homestead. Strashok became a successful farmer.

Educated in St. Michael, Strashok attended the Vermillion School of Agriculture, graduating in 1927. Strashok then continued his education becoming a student at the University of Alberta. He obtained a degree in Science in 1933. After graduation, he helped his father run the family farm.

Fred Strashok unsuccessfully ran as the U.F.A. candidate for the provincial Victoria constituency in 1935.

STRINGAM, George Lewis

Born May 7, 1876 in Holden, Utah, son of pioneer stock George W. Stringham and Emily Billings. Educated in Utah schools, Stringham attended the Brigham Young Academy at Provo. As a young man, he worked as a cowboy on a ranch in southern Utah and served on a mission in Australia. He served as a Democratic Senator in the Utah State Legislature from 1900 to 1908.

After moving to Alberta in 1910, Stringham farmed in Glenwood and became active in the United Farmers of Alberta Movement.

George Lewis Stringham ran as the U.F.A. candidate,

successfully winning the provincial seat from Cardston in 1921. He sat in the Legislature for 14 years as private member on the government side of the provincial House. In the 1935 St. Albert election, Stringham placed second, losing to Social Creditor N. Eldon Tanner by 1,462 votes. Stringham forfeited his deposit. After his loss, Stringham retired from politics to his ranch. When he retired from ranching, George L. Stringham moved to Lethbridge, Alberta.

In 1906, he married Sarah Williams, daughter of Sylvester Williams. They had nine children, including Bryant Stringham, Bryce Stringham and Mark R. Stringham. All of their children were active in politics. Bryce Stringham was returned as the Liberal member for the provincial Bow Valley – Empress constituency in 1955.

George L. Stringham died July 4, 1959 in Lethbridge, at the age of eighty-three.

TOBIN, Stanley Gilbert

Born January 19, 1871 in Bridgewater, Nova Scotia, son of James Tobin and Mary Ellen MacDonell.

Educated at the Bridgewater Academy, Preton and Truro, Tobin qualified as a teacher. For a number of years, he taught at the Lunenburg Academy.

Tobin came to the District of Alberta, N.W.T. in 1904, where he settled at Leduc and he became a schoolteacher. Later, Tobin became a prominent Leduc businessman and served on the Municipal Council and School Board.

A Liberal, Stanley C. Tobin successfully contested Leduc in 1913. He was re-elected in 1917 and 1921 – he won the latter election by ten votes. He sat in the Legislature for twelve years. In 1925, Tobin resigned his seat.

On the Federal scene, Stanley F. Tobin, running as a Liberal, successfully contested the Wetaskiwin riding in the 1925 general election. He defeated U.F.A. candidate D.W. Warner by a 228-vote margin. Tobin sat in Parliament for one year, being defeated in his re-election bid in the 1925 federal election.

That year, Tobin left Alberta and settled in Toronto where he became a Mining Executive. He was President of Glenora Gold Mines and Vice President of Nicholson Mines for many years.

Stanley Gilbert Tobin died June 12, 1948 in Toronto at the age of seventy-seven.

TURNER, Miss Amelia

Born on February 11, 1894 in Tottenham, Ontario. A long time resident of Calgary, Miss Turner (no relation of W.E. Turner) was the advertising manager of The U.F.A., the official publication of the large farm organization in the early 1930's. Miss Amelia Turner was also active in the Trade Union Movement and in civic politics.

Interested in provincial politics, Miss Amelia Turner, running as a Labor candidate, twice unsuccessfully contested Calgary by-elections. Her first attempt was during January 1933. The vacancy was caused by the death of George H. Webster. She placed second, losing to Norman Hindsley. Again in January 1934, as the C.C.F. and Canadian Labor Party candidate, Turner was unsuccessful in the by-election. This vacancy was caused by the resignation of Conservative Dr. H.W. McGill on his acceptance of a federal government appointment. Miss Turner again placed second, losing to Liberal, W.H. Ross.

WALKER, Gordon Beverly

Born March 22, 1891 in Camlachie, Ontario, son of Henry Walker and Rachel A. Mathews. Educated at Pipestone, Manitoba, Walker attended Winnipeg's Manitoba Agricultural College, graduating with a Science degree.

Coming to Alberta in 1920, he became a livestock instructor and farm manager of the Clarasholm School of Agriculture. Walker held this position for four years and then became a farmer.

Gordon B. Walker was returned as the U.F.A. member for the provincial Clarasholm constituency in 1926. He sat in the Legislature for nine years.

In 1935 he was awarded the King George V. Jubilee Medal.

G.B. Walker died in July, 1953.

(See: The Canadian Who's Who, 1936-1937)

WALKER, James H.

Born May 31, 1885 in Coalville, Summit County, Utah.

Coming to the District of Alberta, N.W.T. as a young man in 1903, Walker settled in Grassy Lake. Two years later, he returned to the United States and worked in the coal industry. However, in 1907, Walker went to the Netherlands as a Mormon missionary. On his return, he settled in Raymond; the center of the new sugar beet development. Walker became the local manager for the Knight Sugar Company, a position he held for many years. He also acquired land of his own which he farmed. Walker took a keen interest in horticulture, and did valuable experimental work with fruit trees in southern Alberta.

An active member of the Mormon Church, Walker served as Bishop of the Raymond Ward. He also served as School Trustee for several years.

Prominent in the United Farmers of Alberta movement, James Walker unsuccessfully ran for the provincial Warner constituency in 1935, being defeated by Social Credit teacher Solon Low. However, in 1940, Walker defeated Low, running this time as an Independent candidate. He sat for one term in the Legislature and for one session as House Leader of the large Independent group. In January 1944, he was named the Alberta leader of the Independents, edging out Mayor Elton of Lethbridge. In the August 1944 general election, Walker was defeated in his re-election bid against Low.

In 1912 he had married Fanny Harris of Layton, Utah and they had 14 children. James Walker died December 14, 1954 in Raymond at the age of sixty-nine.

WARNER, Daniel Webster

Born 1857 in Richland, Iowa, U.S.A., son of Gideon W. Warner and Matilda. Warner was educated in both Iowa and Nebraska.

Daniel Warner came to the District of Alberta, N.W.T. in 1900, and became a well-known south Edmonton farmer and stock raiser. He was also an active member of the United Farmers of Alberta movement.

Daniel Webster Warner unsuccessfully ran as a Liberal for the federal Strathcona riding in 1917. He was returned as the U.F.A. member for the federal Strathcona riding in 1921. In 1925 he was defeated by Liberal Stanley G. Tobin.

Warner died in May of 1933, in Edmonton.

WASHBURN, Willard Moody

Born September 12, 1875 in Argyle, Lee County, Iowa, U.S.A., son of Philander S. Washburn and Minnie Stanwood. Washburn was of English descent and educated in his hometown of Argyle. Leaving the United States, he came to Alberta and became a well-known Stony Plain farmer.

Willard M. Washburn was returned as the U.F.A. member for the provincial Stony Plain constituency in 1921. He sat in the Legislature for 14 years as a private member on the government side of the chamber.

WHEATLEY, Jonathan M.

During World War I, he enlisted in the Canadian Army, and saw active service on the Western Front.

After being demobilized, Wheatley joined a group of other returned soldiers to form a farming colony near Chancellor. He became a prominent farmer and active in the U.F.A. movement. Notably, Wheatley served as the President of the U.F.A. Bow Valley branch for many years.

Jonathan M. Wheatley unsuccessfully ran for the provincial Bow Valley constituency in 1935.

WOOD, Henry Wise

Born in 1860 on a farm near Monroe City, Missouri, he was

the son of John Oliver Wood, a prosperous slave-owning farmer who served in the Confederate Army during the American Civil War. Wood attended the Christian University in Canton, Missouri, preparing for the ministry in the Campbellite sect. Though he did not enter the ministry, his study of the Bible and especially the social teaching of Christ, exerted a profound influence on his thinking.

Wood tilled the soil in his home state and then migrated to Texas where he became a cotton planter. Returning to Missouri, he again engaged in farming. His tuition in agrarian politics was largely obtained in the Farmers' Equity Movement in the mid-west in the 1980s.

Attracted to Canada in 1905, Wood, at the age of forty-five, obtained a farm in the Carstairs district of central Alberta. However, he never gave up his American citizenship. Henry Wood became actively interested in the farmers' movement in his community. In 1909 he joined the recently organized United Farmers of Alberta and became the U.F.A. President seven years later. In 1917 Prime Minister Borden asked him to join the Union government as Minister of Agriculture. Wood refused.

It was under his careful guidance that the farmers' political movement developed in Alberta. After the provincial election of 1921, U.F.A. candidates had won a total of 39 seats in the 60 member Legislature. Although Wood was offered the premiership, Herbert Greenfield was unexpectedly chosen to be the Premier by the U.F.A. members of the Legislature.

Henry Wise Wood was the most outstanding figure, politically and economically, that the agrarian movement in Western Canada produced. He was the directing spirit of the U.F.A. until his retirement from the presidency in 1931. By virtue of his position, he was often described as exercising a subtle but beneficent "dictatorship" in regards to his relations with the farmers' government in Edmonton.

Some 30,000 Alberta farmers united into a solid group under Wood's leadership and wielded tremendous power as a "class" group. The U.F.A. dominated provincial politics for fourteen years until the Social Credit were swept into office in 1935. A strong believer in co-operation, he was Chairman of the Alberta Wheat Pool from 1923 to 1937. The University of Alberta conferred upon him the honorary degree of Doctor of Laws in 1929.

Wood died at the age of eighty-one in Calgary in 1941. Though he was never elected to either the Legislature or the federal Parliament, H.W. Wood was referred to as "The Moses of the Alberta Farmers."

He died June 10, 1941 in Calgary.

WRIGHT, Charles O.F.

Born in 1873 in Simcoe County, near Barrie, Ontario, son of English-Irish parentage. Wright was educated in Barrie, Ontario.

He came to Alberta as a young man and worked at a variety of jobs. Finally he settled near Hughenden and became a prominent farmer. Active in community affairs, he served for eight years as the Secretary-Treasurer of the Eastervale School Board. He was also active in the United Farmers of Alberta movement.

Charles O.F. Wright was returned as the member for the provincial Ribstone constituency in 1931. He defeated the Liberal incumbent James A. Turgeon, with a majority of 1,300 votes. Despite the sweeping support, Wright sat in the Legislature for only part of the 1922 session.

Charles Wright died March 28, 1922 in Edmonton, while still a sitting member at the age of forty-nine. He was a hard working member of the Legislature. (He was former Premier Charles Stewart's brother-in-law.)

Board of Directors
of the
United Farmers of
ALBERTA
(1921)

(Indicates they became M.L.A.s) *

PRESIDENT: Henry Wise Wood, Carstairs
VICE-PRESIDENTS: Percival Baker, * Ponoka
PROVINCIAL: * Herbert Greenfield
SECRETARY: H. Higginbotham, Calgary

MEMBERS"

* George Bevington * Winterburn Cand
* F.W. Bredin, Peace River M.L.A.
* G.A. Forster, NATEBY M.L.A.
* R.L. Gaetz, Red Deer Cand
C.H. Harris, Oyen
S. Lunn, Pincher Creek
C.H. McFarquhar, Cremone
* Lawrence Peterson, * Taber
Rafn
G. Roose
H. E. G. H. Scholefield, Crossfield Cand
S.S. Sears, Nanton
* D.W. Warner, * Edmonton MP

WOMEN'S BRANCH (U.F.A.W.):

PRESIDENT: Mrs. O.S. Sears, Nanton

PAST PRESIDENT: * Mrs. M. Irene Parleby, * Pono
LACOMBE
VICE-PRESIDENT: Mrs. R.G. Gunn, Paradise Valley

Mrs. O.S. Welch, Gleichen

U.F.A. SOLICITOR: * John E. Brownlee, * Calgary

Birth Place	Previous Occupation	Final Occupation
ALLEN, Hugh Wright Ontario	Chemist	Farmer
ANDREWS, Albert George England	Teacher	Farmer
ANGELO, John Italy	Farmer	-
AXELSON, Carl Henning Sweden	Trade Union	Farmer
BAILEY, William American	Timber Worker	Farmer
BAKER, Percival Ontario	Preacher	Farmer
BAKER, Perrin Earle Ontario	Preacher	Farmer
BEVINGTON, George Elza American	Miner	Farmer
BOUTILLIER, Arthur Moreu Nova Scotia	Farmer	-
BRETON, Douglas Corney S. Africa	Farmer	-

BROWNLEE, John Edward Ontario	Teacher	Lawyer
BUCKLEY, John Charles Ireland	Poor Law Administration	Farmer
CAMERON, Donald Scotland	Carpenter	Farmer
CARSON, Samuel Allen Ontario	Farmer	-
CHORONOHUS, Michael Russia	Farmer	-
CLAYPOOL, Austin Bingley American	Farmer	-
CONNER, Maurice Joy American	Preacher	Farmer
COOK, Earl Goodwin Ontario	Farmer	-
COOK, John Ernest Ontario	Teacher	Farmer
COOTE, George Gibson Ontario	Farmer	-
COURSIER, Dr. Heber Leon Br. Columbia	Dentist	Farmer
CULLE, James M.	Farmer	

DESLISLE, John Amos American	Merchant	Farmer
ENZENAUER, Peter American	Miner	Farmer
EVANS, John P. England	Lumber Comp.	Proprietor
FARQUHARSON, William George Ontario	Pharmacist	Farmer
FEDUN, William Phillip Poland	Horticulturalist	Farmer
FIELD, Mrs. Jean Hunter (nee John)	House Wife	
FORSTER, Gordon Alexander Ontario	University educated	Farmer
FRAME, John W. Scotland	Liberal MLA	Farmer
GAETZ, Raymond L. Nova Scotia	Businessman	
GALBRAITH, Daniel Harcourt Sr. Ontario	University educated	Farmer
GARDINER, Robert Scotland	Farmer	-
GARLAND, Edward Joseph Ireland	University educated	Farmer

GORESKY, Isidore Bukovina		Teacher
GREENFIELD, Herbert England		Farmer
GRISDALE, Frank Sydney Quebec	College Principal	Farmer
HENNIG, Rudolph Russia		Farmer
HOADLEY, George England		Farmer
IRONSIDE, Cyril M. England		Farmer
IRVINE, William Scotland	Preacher	Journalist
JACKSON, William J.		Farmer
JELLIFF, Lincoln Henry American	Lawyer	Farmer
JOHANSEN, John A. American	Teacher	Farmer
JOHNSTON, George Norman Ontario	Teacher	Farmer
JOLY, Joseph Phydime "Laudas" Quebec	Surveyor	Farmer

KELLNER, Donald Ferdinand Ontario		Farmer
KENNEDY, Donald MacBeth Scotland	Educated Preacher	Farmer
KING, Thomas Owen American	Ranch hand	Farmer
LEEDY, John Whitnah American	Governor of Kansas	Kansas
LOVE, George A. American	Minister	Farmer
LOVE, John Russell Ontario	Soldier	Farmer
LUCAS, William Thomas Ontario	College graduate	Farmer
LUCHKOVICH, Michael American	University graduate	Farmer
LYMBUR, John Farquhar Scotland	University graduate	Lawyer
MacLACHLAN, George Scotland	College graduate	Farmer
MACLELLAN, John James Nova Scotia	Blacksmith	Farmer
McCOOL, Robert Milton Manitoba		Farmer

McKEEN, Charles Milton New Brunswick	Soldier	Farmer
McKINNEY, Louise Crummy Ontario	Teacher	
McLEOD, Donald Scotland	College graduate	Farmer
McPHERSON, Oran Leo "Tony" American	College graduate	Farmer
MATHESON, Archibald Malcolm Scotland	Banker	Farmer
MICHALCHEON, George M. Bukovina	Teacher	Merchant
MISKEW, Peter Alexander Poland	Teacher	Lawyer
MONTAINBAULT, Hyacinthe Quebec	Inspector	
MOORE, Alex Ontario		Farmer
MORISSEY, Joseph P. Alberta	University graduate	Farmer
MUIR, D.S.		Farmer
NORMANDEAU, Louis Quebec		Farmer

PARLBY, Mary Irene England	Grandfather was a British MP	Housewife (farmer)
PETERSON, Lawrence American		Farmer
PLUMER, Benjamin Smith American	Implement dealer	Farmer
PROUDFOOT, Lorne Ontario	Teacher	Farmer
PYE, Ronald		Farmer
REID, Richard Gavin Scotland		Farmer
ROBINSON, C.W.		Farmer
RONNING, Chester Alvin China	Lutheran Missionary	College Principal/Farmer
ROSS, Alex Scotland		Stone Mason
ST. ARNAUD, Telespore Quebec		Farmer
ST. GERMAIN, Omer Quebec	University graduate	Lawyer
SANDERS, Albert Leroy American		Farmer

SCHOOLING, Lacky P. American	Minister	Farmer
SHARPE, Major Wallace J. Alberta	Soldier	Farmer
SHIELD, William Hetherington England		Farmer
SMITH, George Wilbert Nova Scotia	Teacher	Farmer
SMITH, Nelson Stuart Manitoba	College instructor	Farmer
SMITH, Vernon Winfield Prince Edward Is.	Railway contractor	Farmer
SMITH, William Cunningham Ontario		Farmer
SPARKS, Evert Ellsworth American		Farmer
SPEAKMAN, Alfred Scotland		Farmer
SPENCER, Henry Elving England	Printer	Farmer
STEVEN, Wilbert Ontario	College graduate	Farmer
STRASHOK, Fred Alberta	University graduate	Farmer

STRINGHAM, George Lewis American	Legislator in Utah	Farmer
TURNER, Miss Amelia	Journalist	
WALKER, Gordon Beverley Ontario		Farmer
WALKER, James H. American	Sugar Beet factory manager	Farmer
WARNER, Daniel Webster American		Farmer
WASHBURN, Willard Moody American		Farmer
WHEATLEY, Jonathan M.	Soldier	Farmer
WOOD, Henry Wise American	Preacher	Farmer
WRIGHT, Charles O.F. Ontario		Farmer

Chart I

Place of Birth:
Alberta = 4
British Columbia = 1
Manitoba = 2
Eastern Canada = 34
(of which Quebec) = 6

Canadian = 41 -> 41

United States = 23
British Isles = 24 -> 47

Eastern = 7
China = 1
South Africa = 1 -> 9

TOTAL 97

Chart II
Occupation When the Individual became active in politics:

Farmers 89
Lawyers 3
Teachers 3
Journalists 2

Former Occupation:

Lawyer 1
Minister/Preacher 6
U.S. Legislator 1
University/ College Graduate 25
Teachers 3
Blacksmith 1
Miner 1
Carpenter 1

ALBERTA ELECTION RETURNS
1921-1935

<u>LIST OF CONSTITUENCIES</u>

1. Acadia
2. Alexandra

3. Athabasca

4. Beaver River
5. Bow Valley

6. Calgary
7. Camrose
8. Cardston
9. Claresholm
10. Clearwater
11. Clover Bar
12. Cochrane
13. Cypress

14. Didsbury
15. Drumheller

16. Edmonton
17. Edson
18. Empress

19. Gleichen
20. Grande Prairie
21. Grouard

22. Hand Hills
23. High River

24. Innisfail
25. Lacombe
26. Lac. Ste. Anne
27. Leduc
28. Lethbridge
29. Little Bow

30. Macleod
31. Medicine Hat

32. Nanton
33. Nanton-Claresholm

34. Okotoks
35. Okotoks-High River

36. Peace River
37. Pembina
38. Pincher Creek
39. Ponoka

40. Redcliffe
41. Red Deer
42. Ribstone
43. Rocky Mountain

44. St. Albert
45. St. Paul
46. Sedgewick
47. Stettler
48. Stony Plain
49. Sturgeon

50. Taber

51. Vegreville
52. Vermillon
53. Victoria

54. Wainwright
55. Warner
56. Wetaskiwin
57. Whitford

ACADIA

1921 LORNE PROUDFOOT U.F.A. 3,106
James Cottrell Liberal 906

1926 LORNE PROUDFOOT U.F.A. 2,056
Dr. J.P. Kerr Conservative 627
George Campbell Liberal 402

1930 LORNE PROUDFOOT U.F.A. 2,103
J.W. Robinson Independent 823

1935 NORMAN B. JAMES Soc. Credit 1,834
Lorne Proudfoot U.F.A. 628
F.W. Beynon Liberal 289

ALEXANDRA

1921 PETER ENZENAUER U.F.A. 2,195
T.H. Currie Liberal 282

1926 PETER ENZENAUER U.F.A. 1,653
I.F. Crossley Conservative 421
Mathew Alsazer Liberal 253

1930 PETER ENZENAUER U.F.A. 1,725
Fred Dunstan Liberal 649

1935 SELMER BERG Soc. Credit 2,479
Peter Enzenauer U.F.A. 924
Norman McClellan U.F.A. 561
T.B. MacKay Conservative 202
C.W. Springfood Communist 197

ATHABASCA

1921 GEORGE MILLS Liberal 1,043
John Angelo 438

1926 JOHN FRAME Liberal 451
J.P. Evans U.F.A. 363

1930 FRANK R. FALCONER Liberal 1,057
John Frame U.F.A. 861

1935 CLARENCE H. TABE Soc. Credit 1,764
A.McLeod Conservative 315
Frank R. Falconer Liberal 950

BEAVER RIVER

1921 JOSEPH M. DECHENE Liberal 1,560
H. Montambault U.F.A. 943

1926 JOHN DELISLE U.F.A. 1,168
Joseph Dechene Liberal 989

1930 CAPT. HARRY DAKIN Liberal 1,021
(on Court recount)
John Delisle U.F.A. 1,028
Luc Lebel Independent 87

1935 LUCIEN MAYNARD Soc. Credit 1,751
Capt. Harry Dakin Liberal 775
John Delisle U.F.A. 572
Walter Allen Conservative 147

BOW VALLEY

1921 CHARLES R. MITCHELL Liberal 1,694
George Love U.F.A. 649

1926 CAPT. JOSEPH T. SHAW Liberal 841
(on final count)
Benjamin S. Plummer U.F.A. 869

1930 JOHN MACKINTOSH Independent 1,253
Lacky P. Schooling U.F.A. 959

1935 WILSON E. CAIN Soc. Credit 1,776
David Nelson Liberal 591
J. Wheatley U.F.A. 401
John MacKintosh Independent 204

CALGARY

1921 ALEX ROSS Labor 7,294
ROBERT C. EDWARDS Independent 6,400
FRED WHITE Labor 6,190
R.C. MARSHALL Liberal 5,426
ROBERT PEARSON Independent 5,141

George H. Webster Liberal 4,391
Clinton J. Ford Liberal 4,230
Robert H. Parkyn Indep. Labor 4,082
Dr. M. C. Costello Conservative 3,808
Charles F. Adams Conservative 3,332
Mrs. F. Langford Liberal 3,282
Dr. Thomas H. Blow Conservative 3,090
Frank S. Selwood Liberal 2,969
Herbert B. Adshead Independent 2,878
F.C. Potts Independent 2,864
E.H. Crandell Conservative 2,663
Mrs. Anne Gale Conservative 2,386

Rev. S.B. Hillocks Conservative 2,282
Frank Williams Labor 1,745
Alex Davidson Independent 1,423

1921 By-election: December 9
ALEX RROSS Labor Acclamation

1923 By-election: January 15
WILLIAM W. DAVIDSON Independent 9,930
Clinton J. Ford Liberal 8,325

1926 A.A. McGILLIVRAY Conservative 5,928
GEORGE H. WEBSTER Liberal 2,941
R.H. PARKYN Indep. Labor 2,467
MRS. NELLIE McCLUNG Liberal 1,928
JOHN IRWIN Conservative 1,662

Alex Ross Labor 1,265
Fred White Labor 1,222
Dr. M.C. Costello Conservative 1,221
R.C. Marshall Liberal 626
J.W. Russell Labor 423
F.C. Potts Independent 54

1930 JOHN IRWIN Conservative 5,520
GEORGE H. WEBSTER Liberal 3,651
JOHN J. BOWLEN Liberal 2,598
FRED WHITE Labor 2,585
HUGH C. FARTHING Conservative 2,279

Harold W. McGill Conservative 1,634
Robert H. Parkyn Independent 1,544
R.H. Weir Liberal 1,191
H.S. Patterson Conservative 1,007
A.C. MacKay Independent 992
W.E. Turner Labor 575
J. O'Sullivan Independent 460

Thomas Vickers Labor 381

1933: By-election: Dr. H.W. McGill vacated his seat
NORMAN HINDSLEY Peoples Pty 12,532
Miss Amelia Turner Labor 10,504
Robert H. Parkyn Indep. Labor 2,003
A.C. MacKay Independent 1,775
J. O'Sullivan Farmer 539
D.R. Crichton Independent 478

1934: By-election: death of Charles Weaver
W.H. ROSS Liberal 10,968
(on final count)
Amelia Turner CCF/CLP 9,065
Charles F. Jamieson Peoples Pty 4,172
Ernest H. Starr Prog. Labor 1,095

1935 ERNEST MANNING Soc. Credit 6,087
FREDERIC ANDERSON Soc. Credit 5,058
JOHN J. BOWLEN Liberal 3,874
MRS. EDITH GOSTICK Soc. Credit 3,787
JOHN W. HUGILL Soc. Credit 3,152
JOHN IRWIN Conservative 2,529

O.G. Devenish Soc. Credit 3,152
Walter Little Soc. Credit 2,963
Hugh C. Farthing Conservative 2,090
Robert H. Weir Liberal 1,774
G.W.H. Millican Liberal 1,566
Fred White Labor 1,024
J.V. Follett Conservative 886
Patrick Lenihan Communist 820
R.W. Watson Liberal 786
Charles F. Jamieson Independent 469
J.V.H. Milvain Conservative 451
A.J.E. Liesemer Labor 449

Robert H. Parkyn Indep. Labor 224
W.G. Southern Labor 172

CAMROSE

1921 V. WINFIELD SMITH U.F.A. 3,040
George P. Smith Liberal 2,391

1921 V. WINFIELD SMITH U.F.A. Acclamation

1926 V. WINFIELD SMITH U.F.A. 3,137
S.M. Westvick Liberal 2,086

1932 By-election: death of V.W. Smith

CHESTER RONNING U.F.A. 2,526
S.M. Westwick Liberal 1,979
Frank P. Layton Conservative 1,101

1935 WILLIAM CHANT Soc. Credit 4,335
J.T. Johnson Liberal 1,395
Chester Ronning U.F.A. 1,039

CARDSTON

1921 GEORGE L. STRINGHAM U.F.A. 1,340
Martin Woolf Liberal 615

1926 GEORGE L. STRINGHAM U.F.A. 1,328
W.H. Caldwell Liberal 598
J.Y. Card Conservative 480

1930 GEORGE L. STRINGHAM U.F.A. 1,364
Ryerson Christie Liberal 825

1935 NATHAN E. TANNER Soc. Credit 2,027

George L. Stringham U.F.A. 565
D.O. Wright Liberal 471

CLARESHOLM

1921 THOMAS C. MILNES Farmer Indep. 809
Louise McKinney U.F.A. 763

1926 GORDON B. WALKER U.F.A. 939
John R. Watt Conservative 422

(see: Nanton-Claresholm)

CLEARWATER

1921 DR. JOHN E. STATE LIBERAL 324
Oliver T. Lee Liberal 147
Robert E. Campbell Conservative 117
S.W. Chambers Independent 60

CLOVER BAR

1930 RUDOLPH HENNIG U.F.A. 1,338
Christian Hein Independent 866
S.T. Bigelow Conservative 692

1935 FLOYD BAKER Soc. Credit 2,503
M.G. Christie Liberal 1,105
David Roberts U.F.A. 844
Septemus Savage Conservative 264

COCHRANE

1921 ALEX MOORE U.F.A. 961
A.S. McDonald Liberal 541

1926 ROBERT MILTON McCOLL U.F.A. 883
William Laut Liberal 597
R.G.C. Mortimer Conservative 385

1930 ROBERT MILTON McCOLL U.F.A. 1,174
William Laut Liberal 1,162

1935 WILLIAM ROBERT KING Soc. Credit 1,880
William Laut Liberal 628
Robert Milton McColl U.F.A. 591
J.A. Tweddle Conservative 337

CORONATION

1921 GEORGE N. JOHNSTON U.F.A. 3,736
Dr. Arthur M. Day Liberal 960

1926 GEORGE N. JOHNSTON U.F.A. 2,387
Dr. Arthur M. Day Liberal 945
A.O. Thomas Conservative 498

1930 GEORGE N. JOHNSTON U.F.A. 2,094
Dr. Arthur M. Day Liberal 1,983

1935 G.L. MacLACHLAN Soc. Credit 2,674
C.C. Wager U.F.A. 844
Robert Densmore Liberal 625

CYPRESS

1926 PERREN E. BAKER U.F.A. 1,220
H.H. Foster Liberal 741
S. Ervine Conservative 175

1930 PERREN E. BAKER U.F.A. 1,315
Robert C. Black Liberal 1,060

1935 AUGUSTUS W. FLAMME Soc. Credit 1,689
Robert C. Black Liberal 789
Perren E. Baker U.F.A. 587
J.H. Duncan Independent 51

DIDSBURY

1921 AUSTIN B. CLAYPOOL U.F.A. 2,528
George H. Webber Liberal 1,734

1926 AUSTIN B. CLAYPOOL U.F.A. 2,292
D. MacDonald Liberal 895
S.P. Williams Conservative 819

1930 AUSTIN B. CLAYPOOL U.F.A. 1,756
W.A. Austin Independent 1,470

1935 EDWARD P. FOSTER Soc. Credit 2,731
Austin B. Claypool U.F.A. 610
A.Sheline Liberal 607
A.S. Gough Conservative 303

DRUMHELLER

1930 FREDERICK C. MOYER Independent 922
A.F. Key Labor
D.A. Macauley Independent 722
John O'Sullivan Communist 188

1935 HERBERT INGREY Soc. Credit 2,158
Frederick C. Moyer Independent 778
Murdock Clark Communist 342
D. McDonald Liberal 341

EDMONTON

1921 A.R. McLENNAN Liberal 6,498
JOHN C. BOWEN Liberal 5,803
NELLIE McCLUNG Liberal 5,388
JOHN R. BOYLE Liberal 5,361
J.W. HEFFERNAN Liberal 5,289

William J. Jackman U.F.A. 4,978
Alfred F. Ewing Conservative 4,777
A.A. Campbell Dom. Labor 3,736
H.H. Crawford Conservative 3,553
Elizabeth Ferris Conservative 3,188
Robert McCreath Dom. Labor 2,931
J.W. Adair Independent 2,571

Elmer E. Roper Dom. Labor 2,515
A.U.G. Bury Conservative 2,509
William A. Wells Conservative 2,329
James K. Cornwall Independent 2,082
A.L. Marks Independent 1,744
Gerald V. Pelton Independent 1,467
William Short Independent 1,447
William R. Ball Indep. Labor 1,409
A.Boileua Conservative 1,226
Mary Cantin Indep. Labor 1,133
Ernest Brown Indep. Labor 1,073
James Bailey Indep. Labor 941
Joe E. White Indep. Labor 927
Marie Mellard Socialist 883

1924 By-election: John R. Boyle vacated his seat when appointed a judge

W.T. HENRY Liberal
Henry M. Bartholomew Labor
Alfred F. Aewing Conservative

Gerard V. Pelton Independent

1926 JOHN F. LYMBURN *U.F.A. 3,046
COL. C.Y. WEAVER *Conservative 2,202
W.W. PREVERY *Liberal 1,517
Joseph A. Clark Independent 1,179
John C. Bowen Liberal 1,147
S.A. Gordon Barnes Independent 1,060
Alfred Farmilo Labor 973
F.G. Follinibee Conservative 881
C. LIONEL GIBBS *Labor 879
W.T. Henry Liberal 858
DAVID M. DUGGAN *Conservative 857
H.H. Crawford Conservative 782
G.W. Findlay Labor 728
Jan Lakeman Labor 605
William Rea Liberal 561
Elmer E. Roper Labor 478
Mark W. Robertson Conservative 361
John W. Leedy Independent 140

*(elected on final count)

1930 JOHN F. LYMBURN U.F.A. 3,230
DAVID M. DUGGAN Conservative 2,665
C. LIONEL GIBBS Labor 2,262
CHARLES Y. WEAVER Conservative 2,013
WILLIAM R. HOWSON Liberal 1,835
DR. W.A. ATKINSON Conservative 1,786

W.W. Prevey Liberal 1,331
J.T.J. Collisson Liberal 1,040
A. Farmilo Labor 832
S.A. Gordon Barnes Labor 818
Jan Lakeman Independent 752
D.K. Knott Labor 745
N.C. Willson Conservative 451

Gerard V. Pelton Liberal 442
J.A. Buchanan Conservative 424
Joseph A. Clarke Independent 374
R.D. Tighe Conservative 189

1931 By-election: death of Col. Charles Yardley Weaver

COL. F.C. JAMIESON Conservative 8,026
Elmer Roper Labor 5,583
John C. Bowen Liberal 2,934
Jan Lakeman Communist 813

1935 WILLIAM R. HOWSON Liberal 9,130
S.A. GORDON BARNES Soc. Credit 4,475
DUNCAN B. MULLEN Soc. Credit 2,500
DAVID M. DUGGAN Conservative 1,496
GEORGE H. VAN ALLEN Liberal 1,255
GERALD O'CONNOR Liberal 1,116

Walter S. Hall Soc. Credit 2,515
John F. Lymburn U.F.A. 2,092
Orvis A. Kennedy Soc. Credit 1,752
Mark W. Robertson Soc. Credit 1,242
Marion Conroy Liberal 1,238
Dr. W.A. Atkinson Conservative 1,210
Jan Lakeman Communist 1,096
Col. F.C. Jamieson Conservative 1,029
G.L. King Soc. Credit 843
J.C.M. Marshall Liberal 673
J.E. Basarab Conservative 671
Walter Morrish Liberal 612
James East Labor 505
Emily L. Fitzimon Conservative 363
J.W. Findlay Labor 331
Elsie Wright Econ. Recon. 192
Carl B. Berg Labor 192
S.S. Bowcott Liberal 166

Alfred Farmilo Liberal 127
D.M. Ramsay Conservative 71
Sidney Parsons Labor 52

EDSON

1921 CHARLES W. CROSS Liberal 1,321
John Diamond 959

1926 CHRISTOPHER PATTINSON Labor 1,116
A.McIntyre Conservative 963
F.J. Doyle Liberal 702

1930 CHRISTOPHER PATTINSON Labor 2,434
Charles E. Payne Liberal 777

1935 JOSEPH UNWIN
J. Cowper Liberal 1,620
Christopher Pattinson Labor 1,414

EMPRESS

1926 WILLIAM C. SMITH U.F.A. 922
Daniel McEachern Liberal 464

D. MacCrimmon Conservative 189

1930 WILLIAM C. SMITH U.F.A. 941
E.A. Montz Independent 617

1935 DAVID LUSH Soc. Credit 1,453
William C. Smith U.F.A. 324
K.A. Pollock Liberal

GLEICHEN:

1921 JOHN CHARLES BUCKLEY U.F.A. 1,565
H. Scott Liberal 1,065

1926 JOHN CHARLES BUCKLEY U.F.A. 1,584
Hugh Miller Conservative 722
Frank Lorent Liberal 48

1930 JOHN CHARLES BUCKLEY U.F.A. 1,566
H.S.B. Chamberlain Independent 1,069

1935 ISAAC M. McCUNE Soc. Credit 2,093
John Charles Buckley U.F.A. 895
V.S. Kingston Liberal 569
Thomas S. Hughes Conservative 439

GRANDE PRAIRIE

1930 HUGH J. ALLEN U.F.A. Acclaimed

1935 WILLIAM SHARPE Soc. Credit 2,741
W. Thompson Liberal 2,387
Hugh J. Allen U.F.A. 1,809
J.S. McKenzie Conservative 464

GROUARD

1921 JEAN-LEON COTE Liberal 963
H.G. Dimsdale Conservative 702

1924 By-election: Cote vacated the seat on his appointment to the Senate.

L. ALCIDAS GIROUX Liberal 1,085
James M. Culle U.F.A. 457

1926 L. ALCIDAS GIROUX Liberal 1,224
H.G. Dimsdale Conservative 407

1930 L. ALCIDAS GIROUX Liberal 1,706
Mrs. Jean Field U.F.A. 1,017

1935 L. ALCIDAS GIROUX Liberal 2,272
R.A. Pelletier Soc. Credit 1,447
E.E. Requier U.F.A. 346

HAND HILLS

1921 GORDON A. FOSTER U.F.A. 4,252
Capt. R.B. Eaton Liberal 1,583

1926 GORDON A. FOSTER U.F.A. 2,665
W.G. Anderson Liberal 778
C.L. Sitlington Conservative 590

1930 GORDON A. FOSTER U.F.A. 2,689
J.L. Newmain Independent 1,507

1935 DR. WALLACE W. CROSS Soc. Credit 3,270
C.W. Robinson U.F.A. 707
William Gibson Liberal 552

HIGH RIVER

1921 SAMUEL BROWN U.F.A. 1,014
John V. Drumheller Liberal 867

1926 SAMUEL BROWN U.F.A. 1,137
Prof. W.L. Caryle Conservative 541
M.R. Morrison Liberal 271

(See Okotoks-High river)

INNISFAIL

1921 DONALD CAMERON U.F.A. 1,661
Daniel Morkeberg Liberal 741

1926 DONALD CAMERON U.F.A. 1,187
Daniel Morkeberg Liberal 844
L.M. McLean Conservative 534

1930 DONALD CAMERON U.F.A. 1,243
Daniel Morkeberg Liberal 878
George Wagner Conservative 604

1935 A.E. MacLELLAN Soc. Credit 2,805
W.H. Stringer Liberal 583
Ronald Pye U.F.A. 306
Arthur A. Stonehouse Conservative 318

LACOMBE:

1921 IRENE PARLBY U.F.A. 2,113
William F. Puffer Liberal 1,539

1926 IRENE PARLBY U.F.A. 1,891
William F. Puffer Liberal 1,162
P.W. Pratt Conservative 476

1930 IRENE PARLBY U.F.A. 1,932
G.R. MacKie Independent 1,830

1935 DUNCAN B. MacMILLAN Soc. Credit 3,483
H.G.S. Sissons Liberal 838

Cyril M. Ironside U.F.A. 721
P.W. Pratt Conservative 519

LAC STE. ANNE

1921 C. MILTON McKEEN U.F.A. 1,574
C.G. Stiles Liberal 837
J.H. McKay

1926 C. MILTON McKEEN U.F.A. 1,757
G. Russell Barker Conservative 492
Henry White Liberal 239

1930 C. MILTON McKEEN U.F.A. acclaimed

1935 ALBERT V. BOURCIER Soc. Credit 1,668
C. Milton McKeen U.F.A. 1,080
Nelles V. Buchanan Liberal 897
Ernest Joly Conservative 133

LEDUC

1921 STANLEY G. TOBIN Liberal 1,351
D.S. Muir U.F.A. 1,341

1926 DOUGLAS C. BRETON U.F.A. 1,961
C.W. Carroll Liberal 1,561
C.B. Kidd Conservative 823

1930 ARTHUR P. MITCHELL Liberal 1,468
Douglas C. Breton U.F.A. 1,408

1935 R. EARL ANSLEY Soc. Credit 2,940
Arthur P. Mitchell Liberal 1,305
J.E. Cook U.F.A. 357
Max von Amerongen Conservative 166

LETHBRIDGE

1921 DR. JOHN S. STEWART Conservative 2,252
John Marsh Labor 1,374

1926 By-election: pending when the Legislature dissolved

ANDREW SMEATON Labor 1,584
R.R. Davidson Conservative 1,459
Dr. W.S. Galbraith Liberal 1,225

1930 ANDREW SMEATON Labor 2,036
W.D. Hardie Independent 1,598
Robert Barrowman Independent 1,005

1935 HANS ENOCH WRIGHT Soc. Credit 3,700
Robert Barrowman Liberal 1,946
Andrew Smeaton Labor 654
George W. Green Conservative 341

LITTLE BOW

1921 O.L. McPHERSON U.F.A. 1,554
James McNaughton Liberal 856

1926 G.L. McPHERSON U.F.A. 1,367
James McNaughton Liberal 556
P.M. Patterson Conservative 475

1930 G.L. McPHERSON U.F.A. Acclamation

1935 REV. PETER DAWSON Soc. Credit 2,322
O.L. McPherson U.F.A. 704
L.H. Stack Liberal 474

MACLEOD

1921 WILLIAM H. SHIELD U.F.A. 727
George Skedding Liberal 620

1926 WILLIAM H. SHIELD U.F.A. 656
J.W. McDonald Liberal 567
Robert Patterson Conservative 156

1930 WILLIAM H. SHIELD U.F.A. 1,539
J.W. McDonald Liberal 800

1935 JAMES HARTLEY Soc. Credit 1,680
W.H. Shield U.F.A. 650
C.T. Schiebout Liberal 387

MEDICINE HAT

1921 PERRIN E. BAKER U.F.A. 4,165
WILLIAM JOHNSON Dominion Labor ,602
Dr. Oliver Boyd Liberal 2,278
H.H. Foster Liberal 2,013

1921 By-election: December 9

PERREN E. BAKER U.F.A. Acclamation

1925 By-election: death of William Johnson

CHARLES PRINGLE Liberal 1,645
Ed McCombs Labor 1,297
J.J. Hendricks Conservative 1,011

1926 CHARLES S. PRINGLE Liberal 1,574
J.J. Hendricks Conservative 1,276

James Hole Labor 718

By-election: death of Charles Pringle
HECTOR LANG Liberal 1,351
J.J. Hendricks Conservative 941
Ed McCombs Labor 810
B.J. Bott Independent 290

1930 HECTOR LANG Liberal 1,774
C.S. Blanchard Conservative 1,150
Isaac Bullivant Independent 935

1935 DR. JOHM L. ROBINSON Soc. Credit 3,236
Hector Lang Liberal 1,252
Isaac Bullivant 653

NANTON

1921 DANIEL H. GALBRAITH U.F.A. 727
John Glendenning Liberal 458

1926 DANIEL H. GALBRAITH U.F.A. 745
Dr. W.H. Keen Conservative 341
Nunham Stanfordd Liberal 204

NANTON-CLARESHOLM

1930 GORDON B. WALKER U.F.A. 1,415
W.J. Ellison Conservative 733

1935 HARRY O. HASLAM Soc. Credit 1,767
Gordon B. Walker U.F.A. 612
C.T. Milnes Liberal 517
H. Stanley Wyatt Conservative 269

OKOTOKS

1921 GEORGE HOADLEY U.F.A. 1,129
E.A Dagget Liberal 390

1921 GEORGE HOADLEY U.F.A. Acclamation

1926 GEORGE HOADLEY U.F.A. 920
W.G. Birney Conservative 850

OKOTOKS – HIGH RIVER

1930 GEORGE HOADLEY U.F.A. 2,834
Malcolm MacGougan Liberal 1,668

1935 REV. W. MORRISON Soc. Credit 3,086
George Hoadley U.F.A. 1,005
A.S. Dick Liberal 970
Victor E. Hessell Conservative 432

OLDS

1921 NELSON STUART SMITH U.F.A. 1,896
Duncan Marshall Liberal 1,238

1926 NELSON STUART SMITH U.F.A. 1,790
Norman E. Cook Liberal 708
L.H. Walkley Conservative 369

1930 FRANK S. GRISDALE U.F.A. 1,790
George Clark Liberal 1,577

1935 HERBERT ASH Soc. Credit 3,538
Dr. A.H. Mann Liberal 935
Frank S. Grisdale U.F.A. 694

William Thomas Conservative 167

PEACE RIVER

1921 DONALD M. KENNEDY U.F.A. 3,291
William A. Rae Liberal 1,336
E.S. Farr 623

1921 By-election: Kennedy vacated his seat

HERBERT GREENFIELD U.F.A. Acclamation

1926 HUGH J. ALLEN U.F.A. 2,548
J.P. McIsaac Liberal 1,131
P.R. McMillan Conservative 965

1930 WILLIAM BAILEY U.F.A. 1,331
C.W. Frederick Independent 795

1935 WILLIAM J. LAMPLEY Soc. Credit 2,269
R.L. Lamont Liberal 1,389
William Bailey U.F.A. 994
"Ged" Baldwin Conservative 308

PEMBINA

1921 GEORGE MacLACHLAN U.F.A. 1,838
Dr. Phillips Liberal 540
David Armitage Conservative 145

1926 GEORGE MacLACHLAN U.F.A. 1,930
E.F. Henderson Liberal 886
A.D. Henderson Conservative 427

1930 GEORGE MacLACHLAN U.F.A. 2,094

H.G. Curlett Independent 1,160

1935 DR. HARRY BROWN Soc. Credit 3,133
H.B. Fraser Liberal 1,145
George MacLachlan U.F.A. 1,030
Maurice Gardam Conservative 183

PINCHER CREEK

1921 EARL G. COOK U.F.A. 572
Harvey Bossenbury Liberal 471
A.E. Cox Independent 192
D.R. McIvor 133

1926 HARVEY BOSSENBURY Liberal 592
Earl G. Cook U.F.A. 542
R.O. Allison 471

1930 HARVEY BOSSENBURY Liberal 959
Earl G. Cook U.F.A. 920

1935 REV. ROY TAYLOR Soc. Credit 1,214
Harvey Bossenbury Liberal 528
R.O. Allison Conservative 312
Earl G. Cook 296

PONOKA

1921 PERCIVAL BAKER U.F.A. 1,391
Dr. W.A. Campbell Liberal 815

1921 By-election: death of Percival Baker

JOHN BROWNLEE U.F.A. Acclamation

1926 JOHN BROWNLEE U.F.A. 1,357

M. Crandell Liberal 453
Arthur Beaumont Conservative 347

1930 JOHN BROWNLEE U.F.A. Acclamation

1935 MRS. EDITH ROGERS Soc. Credit 2,295
John Brownlee U.F.A. 879
Robert McLaren Liberal 696

REDCLIFFE

1921 WILLIAM C. SMITH U.F.A. 1,950
Charles S. Pringle Liberal 1,387

(See: Empress Constituency)

RED DEER

1921 GEORGE W. SMITH U.F.A. 2,160
John J. Gaetz Liberal 1,146
1926 GEORGE W. SMITH U.F.A. 1,450
W. Ernest Payne Conservative 1,329
John J. Gaetz Liberal 621

1930 GEORGE W. SMITH U.F.A. 2,144
W. Ernest Payne Conservative 2,056

1931 By-election: death of George W. Smith

W. ERNEST PAYNE Conservative 1,651
Raymond L. Gaetz U.F.A. 1,491
James Bannerman Liberal 503
F.G. Bray Communist 261

1935 ALFRED HOOKE Soc. Credit 3,565
M.H.W. Fizzell Liberal 788

E.G. Johns Independent 622
W. Ernest Payne Conservative 612
G.H. Palmer Communist 291

RIBSTONE

1921 CHARLES O.F. WRIGHT U.F.A. 2,192
James Turgeon Liberal 909

1922 By-election: death of C.O.F. Wright

W.G. FARQUHARSON U.F.A. 1,596
J.J. McKenna Liberal 408

1926 W.G. FARQUHARSON U.F.A. 1,524
Allan Johnstone Liberal 622
E.G. Tregale Conservative 284

1930 W.G. FARQUHARSON U.F.A. 1,672
James Lee Liberal 837
Daniel Glocksin Liberal 271

1935 ALBERT L. BLUE Soc. Credit 2,684
Raymond M. Lee Liberal 589
W.G. Farquharson U.F.A. 499

ROCKY MOUNTAIN

1921 CHRISTOPHER Labor 1,304
A.Morrison Liberal 1,143
W. Sharpe Independent 811

1926 P.M. Christopher Labor 1,765
John Kerr Conservative 801
A.M. Densmore Labor 786

1930 GEORGE CRUICKSHANK Independent 1,604
Joseph Stabbs Labor 820
"Rock" Sudworth Independent 783

1935 LAWRENCE ERNEST DUKE Soc. Credit 2,996
Harvey Murphy Communist 1,080
Dr. D .J. MacNeil Liberal 1,033
George Cruickshank Independent 389

ST. ALBERT

1921 TELESPHORE ST. ARNAUD U.F.A. 1,234
Lucien Boudreau Liberal 1,000

1926 LUCIEN BOUDREAU Liberal 1,058
Michael Hogan Independent 683
Louis Normandeau U.F.A. 628
J.A. Louiseau Conservative 85

1930 OMER ST. GERMAIN U.F.A. 1,427
Lucien Boudreau Liberal 1,161

1935 CHARLES HOLDER Soc. Credit 1,431
Lucien Boudreau Independent 955
Omer St. Germain Liberal 446
A.S. McRae Independent 258
Joseph P. Morissey U.F.A. 116

ST. PAUL

1921 J.P. LAUDAS JOLY U.F.A. 1,378
P.E. Lessardrd Liberal 984

1926 J.P. LAUDAS JOLY U.F.A. 1,453
H. Montambault Liberal 603

E. McPheeters Indep. Farmer 105

1930 JOSEPH M. DECHENE Liberal 1,653
J.P. Laudas Joly U.F.A. 1,161

1935 JOSEPH BEAUDRY Soc. Credit 2,567
Joseph M. Dechene Liberal 1,963
J.P. Laudas Joly U.F.A. 946

SEDGEWICK

1921 RLES A. STEWART LIBERAL Acclamation

1922 By-election: Charles A. Stewart vacated his seat

ALBERT GEORGE ANDREWS U.F.A. Acclamation

1926 A.G. ANDREWS U.F.A. 2,264
J.H. Caldwell Liberal 694
H.A. Dreany Conservative 468

1930 A.G. ANDREWS U.F.A. 2,265
W.H. Wallace Conservative 828

1935 ALBERT EDWARD FEE Soc. Credit 3,642
A.G. Andrews U.F.A. 833
H.G. Thunell Liberal 632

STETTLER

1921 ALBERT L. SANDERS U.F.A. 3,106
Edward Prudden Liberal 1,608

1926 ALBERT L. SANDERS U.F.A. 2,122

Henry A. Blair Conservative 921
George Auxier Liberal 837

1930 ALBERT L. SANDERS U.F.A. 1,934
Henry A. Blair Conservative 1,147
A.B. Clark Liberal 761

1935 CHARLES COCKROFT Soc. Credit 3,603
M.J. Brennan Liberal 882
Albert L. Sanders U.F.A. 522
Henry A. Blair Conservative 271

STONY PLAIN

1921 WILLARD M. WASHBURN U.F.A. 1,001
J. Miller Liberal 647
Frederick Lundy Conservative 306
Daniel Bronx Independent 47

1926 WILLIAM M. WASHBURN U.F.A. 759
Frederick Lundy Conservative 414
Dr. R. M. Oatway Liberal 368
M. McKinley Indep. Lib. 323

1930 DONALD MACLEOD U.F.A. 1,406
George J. Bryan Liberal 1,247

1935 WILLIAM E. HAYES Soc. Credit 2,832
George J. Bryan Liberal 1,473
Donald Macleod U.F.A. 312
R.C. Johnson Conservative 171

STURGEON

1921 SAMUEL A. CARSON U.F.A. 2,815

John R. Boyle Liberal 1,949

1926 SAMUEL A. CARSON U.F.A 709
J.E. Holmes Conservative 551

1930 SAMUEL A. CARSON U.F.A. 1,406
John Kuzek Liberal 1,129

1935 JAMES M. POPIL Soc. Credit 2,465
Dr. G.J. Hope Liberal 1,533
J. Russell Love U.F.A. 857
G.G. Fowler United Front 361

TABER

1921 LAWRENCE PETERSON U.F.A. 2,309
Archibald J. McLean Liberal 1,991

1926 LAWRENCE PETERSON U.F.A. 1,929
J.J. Horrigan Liberal 709
James Harper Prowse Conservative 551

1930 JOHN J. MACLELLAN U.F.A. 1,848
J.E. Evanson Independent 1,516

1935 JAMES HANSEN Soc. Credit 2,879
John J. MacLellan U.F.A. 757
B.L. Cooke Liberal 642

VEGREVILLE

1921 A.M. MATHESON U.F.A. 3,047
James S. McCallum Liberal 1,325

1926 A.M. MATHESON U.F.A. 1,986

J.D. Hannan Liberal 1,395
A.W. Fraser Conservative 687
P. Buhry Independent 337

1930 A.M. MATHESON U.F.A. 2,364
Harry A. White Liberal 1,757

1935 DR. J. L. McPHERSON Soc. Credit 2,817
C. Gordon Liberal 1,681
A. M. Matheson U.F.A. 995
Michael H. Ponich Conservative 109

VERMILLION

1921 RICHARD GAVIN REID U.F.A. 2,955
A.W. Ebbett Liberal 939

1921 RICHARD GAVIN REID U.F.A. Acclamation

1926 RICHARD GAVIN REID U.F.A. 1,981
W.J. MacNab Conservative 592
A.W. Ebbett Liberal 492

1930 RICHARD GAVIN REID U.F.A. 2,551
Robert B. Hall Liberal 1,522

1935 WILLIAM A. FALLOW Soc. Credit 2,452
A.P. Hunter Liberal 1,062
Richard Gavin Reid U.F.A. 876
William Halina Communist 838
A.E. Williams Conservative 244

VICTORIA

1921 WILLIAM FEDUN U.F.A. 1,401
Frank A. Walker Liberal 1,288

1926 RUDOLPH HENNIG U.F.A. 1,476
Frank A. Walker Liberal 1,243

1930 PETER MISKEW U.F.A. 1,588
S.W. Bahley Liberal 1,522
E. Olendy Independent 47

1935 SAMUEL W. CALVERT Soc. Credit 2,045
C.F. Connolly Liberal 1,181
Fred Strashok U.F.A. 319
V. Kupechenka Conservative 141

WAINWRIGHT

1921 J. RUSSELL LOVE U.F.A. 1,877
Harcus Strachan, VC Liberal 913
George Leroy Hudson Conservative 459

1926 J. RUSSELL LOVE U.F.A. 1,609
George Leroy Hudson Conservative 1,017

J. RUSSELL LOVE U.F.A. 1,446

Ernest A. Pitman Independent 1,005
S.R. Bowerman Liberal 650

1935 WILLIAM MASON Soc. Credit 2,382
Peter Milne Liberal 953
Dr. H.L. Coursier U.F.A. 811
Robert Smallwood Conservative 194

WARNER

1921 MAURICE JOY CONNOR U.F.A. 741

Frank Leffingwell Liberal 490

1926 MAURICE JOY CONNER U.F.A. 741
Frank Leffingwell Liberal 225
Dr. G.N. Giles Conservative 190
1930 MAURICE JOY CONNOR U.F.A. 1,342
Roi W. Risinger Liberal 709

1935 SOLON EARL LOW Soc. Credit 1,702
James H. Walker U.F.A. 588
Frank Leffingwell Liberal 534
H.C. Moir Independent 227

WETASKIWIN

1921 EVERT E. SPARKS U.F.A. 1,508
Hugh J. Montgomery Liberal 1,216

1926 EVERT E. SPARKS U.F.A. 1,274
Hugh J. Montgomery Liberal 1,198
J.E. Inglis Conservative 288

1930 HUGH J. MONTGOMERY Liberal 1,713
Evert E. Sparks U.F.A. 1,417

1935 REV. JOHN WINGBADE Soc. Credit 2,763
Hugh J. Montgomery Liberal 1,149
Wilbert Stevens U.F.A. 506
Robert H. Inglis Conservative 187

WHITFORD
1921 REW SHANDRO Liberal Acclamation

1921 MICHAEL CHORONUS U.F.A. 1,846

Andrew Shandro Liberal 525

1926 GEORGE MIHALCHEON U.F.A. 1,449
Andrew Shandro Independent 373
Nicholas Grekol Liberal 371
E. Michayluk Conservative 274
L.M. Feruson Independent 88

1930 ISIDORE GORESKY U.F.A. 1,799
George Szkwarok Liberal 766
S. Suwala Independent 47

1935 WILLIAM TOMYN Soc. Credit 1,265
Michael Novakowski Communist 966
Isidore Goresky U.F.A. 940
Andrew Shandro Liberal 615

Vice = instead of

Summary of Alberta By-Elections

<u>Calgary</u>

1921 Dec. 9: Alex Ross (LAB)
Re-elected on appointment to Cabinet

1923 Jan. 15: William M. Davidson (IND)
Vice – Robert C. Edwards, decreased

1933 Jan. 9: Norman Hindsley (IND)
Vice – Harold W. McGill, vacated his seat

1934 Jan. 15: William H. Ross (LIB)
Vice – George H. Webster, deceased

<u>Camrose</u>

1932 Oct. 25: Chester A. Ronning (U.F.A.)
Vice – V. Winfield Smith, deceased

Edmonton

1923 Oct. 27: William T. Henry (LIB)
Vice – John R. Boyle, appointed a judge

1931 Jan. 9: Frederick C. Jamieson (CONS)
Vice – Charles Y. Weaver, deceased

Grouard

1924 Jul. 11: Leonidas A. Giroux (LIB)
Vice – Jean L. Cote, appointed to the Senate

Medicine Hat

1921 Dec. 9: Perrin E. Baker (U.F.A.)
Re-elected on his appointment to the Cabinet

1925 Sep. 29: Charles S. Pingle (LIB)
Vice – William C. Johnston, deceased

1928 May 1: Hector Lang (LIB)
Vice – Charles S. Pingle, deceased

Okotoks

1921 Dec. 9: George Hoadley (U.F.A.)
Re-elected on appointment to the Cabinet

Peace River

1921 Dec. 9: Herbert Greenfield (U.F.A.)
Vice – Donald M. Kennedy, vacated his seat to enter federal politics

Ponoka

1921 Dec. 9: John E. Brownlee (U.F.A.)
Vice – Percival Baker, member elect, deceased

Red Deer

1931 Nov. 16: W. Ernest Payne (CONS)
Vice – George W. Smith, deceased

Ribstone

1922 Jul. 10 : William G. Farquharson (U.F.A.)
Vice- Charles O.F. Wright, deceased

Sedgewick

1923 Jul. 10: Albert G. Andrews (U.F.A.)
Vice – Charles A. Stewart, vacated his seat to enter federal politics

Vermillion

1921 Dec. 9: Richard G. Reid (U.F.A.)
Re-elected on appointment to Cabinet

Whitford

1923 Jul. 10: Michael Chornohus (U.F.A.)
Vice – Courts declared previous election void.

Summary of Election Returns for the 1921, 1926, 1930, and 1935 Alberta General Elections

Summary of General Election Returns

1921 Membership 61

Government	MEMBERS	POPULAR VOTE
United Farmers of Alberta	38	29%
Labor (U.F.A. allies)	4	11%
	42	39%

Opposition	MEMBERS	POPULAR VOTE
Liberal	15	34%
Conservative	-	11%
Independents	4	10%
	19	55%

During the term of this Legislature-

1. LIBERALS: died (1-State), resigned (3-Cross, Chas, Steward, Tobin), appointed to the Bench (2- Boyle, Mitchell), appointed to the Senate (1-Cote), the election was declared void and a new writ issued (1-Shandro) for a total of 8.

2. INDEPENDENTS: died (1-Edwards), resigned (1-Edwards) and one resigned (John Stewart) for a total of 2.

(In 1924 the Legislature abolished the Clearwater constituency after the death of its member Dr. J.E. State)

1926 Membership 60

Government	MEMBERS	POPULAR VOTE
United Farmers of Alberta	43	40%

Opposition	MEMBERS	POPULAR VOTE
Liberal	7	26%
Labor	5	8%
Conservative	4	22%
Independent	1	1%
	17	57%

During the term of this Legislature –

1. LIBERAL: died (1-Pringle)

2. Liberals elected 3 French-speaking constituencies (Athabasca, Grouard, St. Albert) one each from Calgary and Edmonton, Medicine Hat and Bow Valley.

3. The Conservatives elected their leader McGillivray and Irwin in Calgary and Duggan and Weaver in Edmonton

4. Labor elected one member from Edmonton, Gibbs, and one from Calgary, White, and one from the 3 coal mining constituencies, Edson, Lethbridge and Rocky Mountain.

5. The Independent/Labor, often referred to as a "socialist" was elected in Calgary Parkyn.

(The Chamber increased by three)

1930 Membership 63

Government	MEMBERS	POPULAR VOTE
United Farmers of Alberta	39	40%

Opposition	MEMBERS	POPULAR VOTE
Liberals	11	25%
Conservatives	6	16%
Labor	4	8%
Independent	3	14%
	24	

NOTE: This year the Federal Conservatives, led by R.B. Bennett of Canada, won the federal general election and formed a minority government.

1. Conservatives elected 3 in Calgary (Farthing, Irwin, McGill) and 3 in Edmonton, and were thereby only an urban party.
2. Labor re-elected one in Calgary (White), and one in Edmonton, and 2 were re-elected in mining constituencies of Edson (Pgattinson) and Lethbridge (Smeaton).
3. Independents were returned in Rocky Mountain (Cruickshank), Bow Valley (McIntosh) and in the new Drumheller constituency (Moyer).
4. Liberals were returned in 3 French speaking northern constituencies (Athabasca – (Falconer), Beaver River (Dakin), and St. Paul (Dechene). St. Germain, the U.F.A. member for St. Albert, crossed the floor of the Chamber to join the Liberals in 1932.

1935 Membership 63

Government	MEMBERS	POPULAR VOTE
Social Credit	56	54%

Opposition	MEMBERS	POPULAR VOTE
Liberal	5	23%
Conservative	2	6%
United Farmers of Alberta	-	11%
	7	

<u>Bow River</u> (est. 1914, altered 1924)

1921 GARLAND, Edward Joseph (P)
1925 GARLAND, Edward Joseph (P)
1926 GARLAND, Edward Joseph (U.F.A.)
1921 GARLAND, Edward Joseph (U.F.A.)
1935 JOHNSTON, Charles Edward (SC)

<u>Calgary East</u>

See Calgary

1921 IRVINE, William (LAB)
1925, DAVIS, Fred (C)
1926 ADSHEAD, Herbert Bealey (L)
1930 STANLEY, George Douglas (C)
1935 LANDERYOU, John Charles (SC)

Calgary West

See Calgary

1921 SHAW, Joseph Tweed (LAB)
1925 BENNETT, Hon. Richard Bedford (C)
1926 BENNETT, Hon. Richard Bedford (C)
1930 BENNETT, Hon. Richard Bedford (C)
*August 25, 1930 BENNETT, Hon. Richard Bedford (C)
1935 BENNETT, Rt. Hon. Richard Bedford (C)

Camrose

See Red Deer and Victoria

1925 LUCAS, William Thomas (P)
1926 LUCAS, William Thomas (U.F.A.)
1930 LUCAS, William Thomas (U.F.A.)
1935 MARSHALL, James Alexander (SC)

Edmonton East

See Edmonton

1917 MACKIE, Henry Arthur (G)
1921 KELLNER, Donald Ferdinand (P)
1925 BURY, Ambrose Upton Gledstanes (C)
1926 BLATCHFORD, Kenneth Alexander (L)
1930 BURY, Ambrose Upton Gledstanes (C)
1935 HALL, William Samuel (SC)

Edmonton West

See Edmonton

1917 GRIESBACH, William Antrobus (G)
1921 KENNEDY, Donald Macbeth (P)
1925 STEWART, Hon. Charles (L)
1926 STEWART, Hon. Charles (L)
*November 2, 1926 STEWART, Hon. Charles (L)
1930 STEWART, Hon. Charles (L)
1935 MacKINNON, James Angus (L)

Lethbridge

See Medicine Hat

1917 BUCHANAN, William Ashbury (O)
1921 JELLIFF, Lincoln Henry (P)
1925 JELLIFF, Lincoln Henry (P)
1926 JELLIFF, Lincoln Henry (U.F.A.)
1930 STEWART, John Smith (C)
1935 BLACKMORE, John Horne (SC)

Macleod

1921 COOTE, George Gibson (P)
1925 COOTE, George Gibson (P)
1926 COOTE, George Gibson (U.F.A.)
1930 COOTE, George Gibson (U.F.A.)
1935 HANSELL, Ernest George (SC)

Medicine Hat

*June 27, 1921 GARDINER, Robert (P)
1921 GARDINER, Robert (P)
1925 GERSHAW, Frederick William (L)

1926 GERSHAW, Frederick William (L)
1930 GERSHAW, Frederick William (L)
1935 MITCHELL, Archibald Hugh (SC)

Peace River

See Edmonton West

1925 KENNEDY, Donald Macbeth (P)
1926 KENNEDY, Donald Macbeth (U.F.A.)
1930 KENNEDY, Donald Macbeth (U.F.A.)
1935 PELLETIER, Rene-Antoine (SC)

Red Deer

1921 SPEAKMAN, Alfred (P)
1925 SPEAKMAN, Alfred (P)
1926 SPEAKMAN, Alfred (U.F.A.)
1930 SPEAKMAN, Alfred (U.F.A.)
1935 POOLE, Eric Joseph (SC)

Strathcona

1921 WARNER, Daniel Webster (P)
See Wetaskiwin

Vegreville

See Victoria

1925 BOUTILLIER, Arthur Moren (P)
1926 LUCHKOVICH, Michael (U.F.A.)
1930 LUCHKOVICH, Michael (U.F.A.)
1935 HAYHURST, William (SC)

Victoria

1921 LUCAS, William Thomas (P)
See Vegreville

Wetaskiwin

See Strathcona

1925 TOBIN, Stanley Gilbert (L)
1926 IRVINE, William (U.F.A.)
1930 IRVINE, William (U.F.A.)
1935 JACQUES, Norman (SC)
Summary of Federal Alberta By-Elections

Medicine Hat

1921 Jun. 27: Robert Gardiner (U.F.A.)
Vice – Arthur L. Sifton, deceased

Edmonton West
1926 Nov. 2: Charles A. Stewart (LIB)
Re-elected on appointment to the Cabinet

Calgary West

1930 Aug. 25: Richard B. Bennet (CONS)
Re-elected on appointment to the Cabinet

Athabasca

1932 Mar. 21: Percy C. Davis (CONS)
Vice - John Buckley, deceased

THE OPPOSITION MEMBERS
1921-1935
(54 individuals)

PLACE OF BIRTH	
Alberta	-
Ontario	23
Manitoba	1
P.E.I.	3
Nova Scotia	2
New Brunswick	1
Quebec	4
Canada	34
United States	2
British Isles	12
Eastern Europe	1

PROFESSION or OCCUPATION

Farmer 10
Lawyer 14
Physician 4
Accountant 1
Printer 2
Merchant –
Businessman 17
Dentist 1
Machinist 1
Druggist 1
Y.M.C.A. 1
Miner 1
Carpenter 1
Writer –
Publisher 3

Dr. William A. Atkinson, Ontario (1876-1948),
Edmonton – Physician
Liberal MLA 1930-1935

Harvey Bossenbury, Ontario (1880-)
Pincher Creek – Merchant/Mayor

Liberal MLA 1926-1935

Lucien Boudreau, Quebec (1875-1962)
St. Albert – Merchant/Hotel Proprietor
Liberal MLA 1926-1930
MLA 1909-1921

John C. Bowen, Ontario (1872-1957)
Edmonton – Minister/educator
Liberal MLA 1921-1926
Lt. Governor of Alberta 1937-1950

John J. Bowlen, P.E.I., (1876-1959)
Calgary – Retired rancher/Bus Driver
Liberal MLA 1930-1944
Lt. Governor 1950-1959

John R. Boyle, Ontario (1871-1936)
Edmonton – Lawyer/alderman
Liberal MLA 1905-1924
Judge 1924-1936

Phillip Martin Christopher, British Isles (1871-1946)
Rocky Mountain – Miner
Labor MLA 1921-1930

Jean-Leon Cote, Quebec (1867-1924)
Grouard – Surveyor
Liberal MLA 1909-1923
Senator 1923

Charles W. Cross, Ontario (1872-1928)
Edson – Lawyer/attorney general
Liberal MLA 1913-1925
MP 1925-1926
Edson MLA, 1913-1917

George E. Cruickshank, Ontario (1877-   )
Rocky Mountain – Merchant
Conservator MLA 1930-1935

Capt. Harry H. Dakin, Nova Scotia (1871-1956)
Beaver River – Sea Captain/Homesteader
Liberal MLA 1930-1935

William M. Davidson, Ontario (1872-1942)
Calgary – Publisher: "The Albertan"
Independent MLA 1917-1921
1923-1926

Joseph M. Dechene, Quebec (1879-1962)
Beaver River – Merchant/agent
Liberal MLA 1921-1926
1930-1935
MP 1940-1958

David M. Duggan, British Isles (1879-1942)
Edmonton – Investment dealer/Alberta cons. Leader
Conservator MLA 1926-1942
Alberta Conservator Leader 1930-1942

Robert Chambers Edwards, British Isles (1864-1922)
Calgary – Publisher: "The Calgary bye opener"
Independent MLA 1921-1922

Frank R. Falconer, American (1883-1970)
Athabasca – Merchant
Liberal MLA 1930-1935

Hugh C. Farthing, Ontario (1892-1968)
Calgary – Lawyer
Conservator MLA 1930-1935

John W. Frame (1871-1932)

Athabasca
Liberal MLA 1926-1930
U.F.A. candidate in 1930

C. Lionel Gibbs, British Isles (1877-1934)
Edmonton – Architect/teacher
Labor MLA 1926-1934

L. Alcidas Giroux, Quebec (1885-1936)
Grouard – Edmonton Lawyer
Liberal MLA 1924-1936

Jeremiah Heffernan, Ont. (1884-1969)
Edmonton – Lawyer/publisher of The Western Catholic
Liberal MLA 1921-1926

William T. Henry, P.E.I. (1872-1952)
Edmonton – Merchant/Mayor
Mayor 1921-1923
Liberal MLA 1924-1926

Norman Hindsley, British Isles (1886-1966)
Calgary – Chartered Accountant
Independent MLA 1933-1935

William R. Howson, Ontario (1883-)
Edmonton – Lawyer/Alberta Liberal Leader
Alberta Liberal leader
MLA 1930-1936
Justice of Supreme Court 1936

John Irwin, Ontario (1869-1948)
Calgary – Merchant/grocer
Conservator MLA 1926-1940

Col. Frederick C. Jamieson, Ont (1875-1966)
Edmonton – Lawyer/ Boer War Veteran

Conservator MLA 1931-1935

Hector Lang, Ontario (1871-1952)
Medicine Hat – Businessman/Mayor
Liberal MLA 1928-1935

Robert C. Marshall, Ontario (1883-1962)
Calgary – Businessman
Liberal MLA 1921-1926

John MacKintosh, British Isles (1890-)
Bow Valley – Businessman
Independent MLA 1930-1935

Nellie McClung, Ontario (1873-1951)
Edmonton – Writer
Liberal MLA 1921-1926

Dr. Harold W. McGill,
Calgary – Physician
Conservator MLA 1930-1932
Federal civil servant 1932

Alexander A. McGillivray, Ontario (1884-1940)
Calgary – Lawyer
Conservator MLA 1926-1930
Justice 1931

Andrew R. McLennan (1871-)
Edmonton – Merchant
Liberal MLA 1921-1925

George Mills, Ontario (1876-)
Athabasca – Farmer
Liberal MLA 1920-1926

Thomas L. Milnes (1870-1954)

Claresholm – Farmer
Independent MLA 1921-1926

Arthur P. Mitchell British Isles (1880-)
Leduc – Farmer
Liberal MLA 1930-1935

Charles R. Mitchell, New. Bruns. (1872-1942)
Bow Valley – Lawyer
Liberal MLA 1910-1925

Hugh J. Montgomery, P.E.I. (1876-1956)
Wetaskiwin – Merchant
Liberal MLA 1914-1921
1930-1935

Frederick C. Moyer,
Drumheller – Lawyer
Independent MLA 1930-1935

Robert Parkyn, British Isle (1862-)
Calgary – Carpenter/alderman
Ind. Labor MLA 1930-1935

Christopher Pattinson, British Isles (1885-)
Edmonton – Miner
Labor MLA 1926-1935

W. Ernest Payne, Ontario (1878-1943)
Red Deer – Lawyer
Conservator MLA 1931-1935

Capt. Robert Pearson, Ontario (1879-1956)
Calgary – Y.M.C.A.
Independent MLA 1917-1926

Warren W. Prevey, American (1874-1949)

Edmonton – Businessman
Liberal MLA 1926-1930

Charles S. Pringle, Manitoba (1880-1928)
Medicine Hat – Druggist
Liberal MLA 1913-1921
1925-1928

William H. Ross,
Calgary
Liberal MLA 1934-1935

Andrew S. Shandro, East Europe (1884-)
Whitford – Farmer
Liberal MLA 1913-1922

Andrew Smeaton British Isles (1879-)
Lethbridge – Machinist
Labor MLA 1926-1935

Dr. Joseph Ephraim State, Ontario (1867-1923)
Clearwater – Physician
Liberal MLA 1917-1923

Charles Allen Stewart, Ontario (1868-1946)
Sedgewick – Farm
Liberal MLA 1909-1923
MP 1926-1935

Dr. John S. Stewart, Ontario (1878-1976)
Lethbridge – Dentist/Soldier
Independent MLA 1911-1925
MP 1930-1935

Stanley G. Tobin, Nova Scotia (1871-)
Leduc- Businessman
Liberal MLA 1913-1925

MP 1925-1926

Col. Charles Y. Weaver, Brit. Isles (1884-1931)
Edmonton – Lawyer/Soldier
Conservator MLA 1926-1931

George H. Webster, British Isles (1873-1934)
Calgary – Merchant
Liberal Mayor 1923-1926
MLA 1926-1934

Fred James White, Ontario (1886-1967)
Calgary – Printer
Labor MLA 1926-1935

ELECTION RETURN FROM FEDERAL ALBERTA RIDING 1921-1935

Acadia

29-10-1925 Robert Gardiner U.F.A. 5,362
Robert B. Eaton L 1,552
George H. Wade C 1,481

14-9-1926 Robert Gardiner U.F.A. 7,041
George H. Wade C 1,803

28-7-1930 Robert Gardiner U.F.A. Accl.

14-10-1935 Victor Quelch SC 6,166
Robert Gardiner U.F.A. 1,859
Arthur M. Day L 1,444
Cyril A. Coughlin C 1,024

Athabasca

29-10-1925 Charles W. Cross L 5,078

Donald F. Kellner U.F.A. 3,648
Charles H. Gauvreau C 1,634

14-9-1926 Donald F. Kellner U.F.A. 4,870
Charles W. Cross L 2,770

28-7-1930 John F. Buckley L 5,527
Donald F. Kellner U.F.A. 4,266
Emmanuel Mihaljuk C 2,218

21-3-1932 Percy G. Davis C 4,910
By-election Isaac S. Doze L 4,096
Louis Normandeau U.F.A. 3,418
Carl Axelson FUL 2,388

14-10-1935 Percy J. Rowe SC 5,424
James O. McNamee L 3,007
Adeodat Boileau C 1,269
J. McRae Newman TECH 733

Battle River

6-12-1921 Henry E. Spencer U.F.A. 2,247
John W.G. Morrison C 1,726
Henry V. Fieldhouse L 1,397

29-10-1925 Henry E. Spencer U.F.A. 5,067
Raymond McFarland Lee L 1,690
John W.G. Morrison C 1,634

14-9-1926 Henry E. Spencer U.F.A. 5,597
John W.G. Morrison C 1,985

28-7-1930 Henry E. Spencer U.F.A. 6,874
John W.G. Morrison C 3,927

14-10-1935 Robert Fair SC 7,029

Henry E. Spencer U.F.A. 3,105
Martin L. Forster L 1,812
John W.G. Morrison C 1,614

Bow River

6-12-1921 Edward J.Garland U.F.A. 11,527
William R. Fulton C 3,579
Herbert A. Wiertz I 369

29-10-1925 Edward J. Garland U.F.A. 3,773
Jesse E. Gouge L 2,917
William J. Douglass C 2,075

14-9-1926 Edward J. Garland U.F.A. 5,144
Acle C. Scratch I 3,028

28-7-1930 Edward J. Garland U.F.A. 5,825
Dawson Graham C 5,653

14-10-1935 Charles E. Johnston SC 7,365
Andrew Davidson L 3,050
Edward J. Garland U.F.A. 2,291
C. Ross Walrod C 1,231

Calgary East

6-12-1921 William Irvine LAB 6,135
Arthur L. Smith C 5,237
Duncan M. Marshall L 3,684

29-10-1925 Fred Davis L 5,560
William Irvine LAB 3,710
William M. Davidson L 2,519

14-9-1926 Herbert B. Adshead L 6,703
Fred Davis C 5,137

William E.W. Guy I 162

28-7-1930 George D. Stanley C 11,344
Herbert B. Adshead 6,002

14-10-1935 John C. Landeryou SC 7,311
George D. Stanley C 5,109
Joseph T. Shaw L 2,138
Edith Patterson CCF 948

Calgary West

6-12-1921 Joseph T. Shaw LAB 7,369
Richard B. Bennett C 7,353
Edward F. Ryan L 1,351

29-10-1925 Richard B. Bennett C 10,256
Joseph T. Shaw LAB 6,040

14-9-1926 Richard B. Bennett C 8,951
Harry W. Lunney L 6,502

28-7-1930 Richard B. Bennett C 13,859
Colin C. McLaurin L 5,787

25-8-1930 Richard B. Bennett C Accl
By-election

14-10-1935 Richard B. Bennett C 9,172
Robert Reid SC 5,817
Peter L. Hyde L 2,130
Henry M. Horrick CCF 686
Charles T. Galbraith, mc. RECONS 411

Camrose

6-12-1921 William T. Lucas U.F.A. 11,402

Christopher F. Connolly L 1,780
James B. Holden C 907

29-10-1925 William T. Lucas U.F.A. 4,204
John W. Thomas L 1,885
Albert Scott C 1,409

14-9-1926 Willam T. Lucas U.F.A. 5,100
Daniel McIvor L 3,490

28-7-1930 William T. Lucas U.F.A. 6,462
Daniel R. McIvor L 4,432

14-10-1935 James A. Marshall SC 8,776
George P. Smith L 2,438
William T. Lucas U.F.A. 2,051

Edmonton East

6-12-1921 Donald F. Kellner U.F.A. 6,094
Joseph A. Clark L 4,147
Henry A. Mackie C 3,139

29-10-1925 Ambrose U.G. Bury C 3,927
Andrew R. McLennan L 3,440
George Latham LAB 2,767

14-9-1926 Kenneth A. Blatchford L 5,090
Ambrose U.G. Bury C 4,925
Jan Lakeman COMM 1,441

28-7-1930 Ambrose U.G. Bury C 6,662
Kenneth A. Blatchford L 4,921
George Latham LAB 2,767
Jan Lakeman COMM 509

14-10-1935 William S. Hall SC 5,721

George B. McLeod L 4,889
Peter E. Bowen C 2,827
Elmer E. Roper CCF 1,726
Oliver C. Doolan COMM 671
Raymond C. Ghostley SC 378

Edmonton West

6-12-1921 Donald M. Kennedy U.F.A. 10,011
Frank Oliver L 8,603
Robert E. Campbell C 4,441

29-10-1925 Charles A. Stewart L 6,394
James M. Douglas C 4,706
James East LAB 2,007

14-9-1926 Charles A. Stewart L 7,223
Frederick C. Jamieson C 5,772

2-11-1926 Charles A. Stewart L Accl.
By-election

28-7-1930 Charles A. Stewart L 9,223
Frederick C. Jamieson C 8,960

17-10-1935 James A. McKinnon L 6,477
James H. Ogilvie C 4,781
James A. Reid SC 3,768

Lethbridge

6-12-1921 Lincoln H. Jelliff U.F.A. 4,961
Martin F. Finn LAB 3,170
Walter S. Ball C 1,328
James E. Lovering L 615

29-10-1925 Lincoln H. Jelliff U.F.A. 5,399

John S. Stewart C 4,656

14-9-1926 Lincoln H. Jelliff U.F.A. 5,138
Andrew B. Hogg C 3,435

28-7-1930 John S. Stewart C 4,863
Thomas O. King U.F.A. 3,880
Arthur G. Baalim L 3,779

14-10-1935 John H. Blackmore SC 6,516
John S. Stewart C 2,990
Lynden E. Fairbairn L 2,109

Macleod

6-12-1921 George G. Coote U.F.A. 6,086
Hugh M. Shaw C 1,767
James Fairhurst LAB 1,407
Joseph E. Gillis L 922

29-10-1925 George G. Coote U.F.A. 4,943
John Herron C 4,239
Thomas C. Milnes L 1,941

14-9-1926 George G. Coote U.F.A. 6,840
John Herron C 3,465

28-7-1930 George G. Coote U.F.A. 6,897
Joseph D. Matheson C 6,105

14-10-1935 Ernest G. Hansell SC 7,028
George G. Coote U.F.A. 3,577
John W. Matthewson C 2,100
Frank O. McKenna I 1,761

Medicine Hat

27-6-1921 Robert Gardiner U.F.A. 13,133
By-election Nelson Spencer C 3,369

6-12-1921 Robert Gardiner U.F.A. 10,295
Frederick W. Gershaw L 2,698

14-9-1925 Frederick W. Gershaw L 4,383
Gilbert M. Blackstock C 2,397
Hugh C. McDaniel U.F.A. 2,039

29-10-1926 Frederick W. Gershaw L 4,206
Gilbert M. Blackstock C 2,226
Carl H. Axelson U.F.A. 2,081

28-7-1930 Frederick W. Gershaw L 6,043
Gilbert M. Blackstock C 3,109

19-10-1935 Archibald H. Mitchell SC 6,371
Frederick W. Gershaw L 3,957
Gilbert M. Blackstock C 9,439

Peace River

29-10-1925 Donald M. Kennedy U.F.A. 3,986
James A. Collins C 3,969
William A. Rae L 3,944
14-9-1926 Donald M. Kennedy U.F.A. 5,323
James A. Collins C 4,398
Joseph A. Clarke L 2,642

28-7-1930 Donald M. Kennedy U.F.A. 10,204
John E. Thompson L 8,930

14-10-1935 Rene-Antoine Pelletier SC 5,513
Joseph P. McIsaac L 3,546
Donald M. Kennedy U.F.A. 1,646
Ernest V. Bergin C 869

Red Deer

6-12-1921 Alfred Speakman U.F.A. 10,849
John F. Day C 2,644
William W.B. McInnes L 2,207

29-10-1925 Alfred Speakman U.F.A. 3,851
Thomas McKercher L 2,462
Joseph J. La France C 2,029

14-9-1926 Alfred Speakman U.F.A. 5,603
Joseph J. La France C 2,151

28-7-1930 Alfred Speakman U.F.A. 6,256
William J. Botterill L 4,571

14-10-1935 Eric J. Poole SC 7,901
George Clark L 1,861
Alfred Speakman 1,855
Arthur H. Stewart C 1,648

Strathcona 6-12-1921 Daniel W. Warner U.F.A. 7,319
James M. Douglas C 2,925
Rice Sheppard L 1,078

Vegreville

29-10-1925 Arthur M. Boutillier U.F.A. 5,103
Charles Gordon L 2,643

14-9-1926 Michael Luchkovich U.F.A. 4,106
Joseph S. McCallum L 3,378

28-7-1930 Michael Luchkovich U.F.A. 5,510
Charles Gordon L 4,606

14-10-1935 William Hayhurst SC 5,124
Michael Luchkovich U.F.A. 3,626
Matthew Popovich COMM 2,001
Joseph B. Holden C 871

Wetaskiwin

29-10-1925 Stanley G. Tobin L 3,429
Daniel W. Warner U.F.A. 3,201
Charles H. Russell C 2,121

14-9-1926 William Irvine U.F.A. 3,897
Stanley G. Tobin L 3,150
Charles H. Russell C 2,243

28-7-1930 William Irvine U.F.A. 4,750
Charles H. Russell C 4,326
William Hayhurst L 2,869

14-10-1935 Norman Jaques SC 7,601
Walter S. Campbell L 2,811
William Irvine U.F.A. 2,772

ERNEST G. MARDON
and
AUSTIN A. MARDON

******

About the Authors

Dr. Ernest G. Mardon was born December 21, 1928, in Houston, Texas, the son of the late Professor Austin Mardon and Marie Dickey. Educated at Gordonstoune, Scotland, he then attended Trinity College, Dublin, before being called up for military service in the Korean War as an officer with the Gordon Highlanders. He came to Canada in 1954 as bureau manager for United Press International, taught high school in Morinville and then did his Doctoral work in Medieval English at the University of Ottawa.

Among the first Faculty of the University of Lethbridge, Dr. Ernest Mardon was also a Visiting Professor at several other Canadian Universities. Dr. Ernest Mardon, *père* and Dr. Austin Mardon, *fils* have produced several works on Alberta political actors. This monograph is their most recent one.

Dr. Austin A. Mardon was born June 25, 1962 in Edmonton, the son of E.G. Mardon and May G. Knowler, an Edmonton teacher. Educated at Lethbridge, he did an M.A. at South Dakota State University and his Ph.D. at Greenwich University, Australia. He then served as a research scientist and participated in a meteorite recovery expedition in the late 1980s spending some 50 days in a two-man tent 10 miles from the South Pole. He is a life member of the New York Explorer's Club.

His main work has been his humanitarian efforts with those suffering from schizophrenia and other mental illnesses.

EDITORS

Mr. Justin Selner

Born December 11, 1990 in Edmonton, Alberta. Justin is a varsity swimmer for the University of Alberta, where he studies Political Science.

-

Mr. Spencer Dunn

Born October 5, 1990 in Fort Saskatchewan, Alberta. Mr. Dunn lives in Edmonton and currently studies Political Science and French at the University of Alberta.

Mr. Emerson Csorba

Born August 12, 1991 in Edmonton, son of Marla and Steven Csorba. Attended Old Strathcona Academic High School and now studies at the University of Alberta.

www.ingramcontent.com/pod-product-compliance
Lightning Source LLC
LaVergne TN
LVHW090946080826
845145LV00003B/907

* 9 7 8 1 8 9 7 4 7 2 1 2 5 *